History
of the
Sandwich Club
of
Raleigh

Raymond L. Murray
and
Jennifer A. Kulikowski

ISBN 978-0-578-08156- 4

Published by
Raymond L. Murray
Raleigh, NC

Printed by Lulu ®
www.lulu.com

TABLE OF CONTENTS

The Sandwich Club of Raleigh

For over 85 years the Sandwich Club has provided fellowship and intellectual challenge to a small group of Raleigh men.

According to Sandwich Club member Carlyle Campbell, both the name and the choice of Thursday nights for meetings were related to the Southern tradition of observing Thursday as "maid's night out," when families were accustomed to having simple suppers in the absence of their cooks. The host club member, instead of imposing on his wife to provide a meal for the meeting, would frequently prepare sandwiches himself or arrange for some other simple menu. Later, though, the meals that preceded the talks by the hosts were by no means as simple as sandwiches. Catering services of the Woman's Club were used and more recently those of the Carolina Country Club and Cypress Retirement Community.

At the start of club operation in 1924, the group met every two weeks, placing a burden on everyone to come up with many topics for presentation. Currently, the club meets once a month on the second Thursday, in nine months of the year, excluding July, August, and December. Thus each member makes about one presentation per year. The host of the dinner meeting prepares and delivers a paper on any subject of interest to him and hopefully his audience. Talks can be on one's experience or based on research on a subject. The chairman calls on each attendee – member or guest – to comment on the occasion and on the paper. Members usually supply additional information based on previous investigation of the announced topic. Often one's prepared comments are anticipated by a prior responder.

Many professions have been represented over the years, including the law, medicine, religion, business, and education. Public servants such as judges, legislators and even State Treasurers have participated.

For many years no alcoholic beverages were served at meetings, but around 1980 Charles Poe broke the ice by offering drinks at his home. Now the group meets at 6:30 PM for cocktails and starts dinner at 7 PM.

The Sandwich Club operates by common consent and tradition, without bylaws. The only two practices of note are the requirement of unanimous acceptance of each new member and a time limit of five minutes for response to a paper.

Recently, the influence of the Sandwich Club in Raleigh has reached the North Carolina Coast. When member Tommy Harrelson moved to Southport, North Carolina, he started an off-shoot of the

Sandwich Club. Harrelson reported, "Our group is appropriately named, 'The River Rats.' We have now 5 members and try to meet once a month. We meet in our homes and cook in and give a program. So the host is responsible for both the cooking and the program. We have a former FBI agent who was also a Seal, a physician, a veterinarian (and the first Republican state senator from our area in about 112 years), a judge, and me. We are a congenial group and we have had varied programs and good food. We will keep it small, since we meet in homes. If we decide to expand, we will need a private room somewhere, and that is not easily available in our village. We have had programs based on bees (Judge Fairley is an amateur bee keeper), anti-terrorism activities (from the former FBI guy), Civil War history and we have a great time."

There is an interesting connection to the 1924 origin of the club provided by current chairman Raymond Murray, who was contemporaneous with founding member Charles Johnson in the period 1957-1962. This can be called "two degrees of separation."

The sections to follow in this monograph include a roster of members with the years their membership started and ended. A total of 81 men have participated. This number seems small, considering the long span of the club's existence, but speaks to the loyalty many members have had to the organization.

The History of the Sandwich Club
By Charles E. Johnson
Presented March 11, 1960

Some lawyer might say that by the way of Confession and Avoidance much should be forgiven the amateur historian and not too much be held against the inexperienced commentator. I was not long in learning that the history of a club such as ours is hard to separate from the roster of members.

Well, Chas., we'll have to do something about that.

It was early in February 1924 that Captain Sam Lawrence galloped into my office, no, the word "gallop" is too strong. It would be better to say, "breezed" into my office with a proposition. It was to be seen from the expression on his face. For Captain Sam enthusiastically embraced new ideas.

This time his idea was appealing, to assemble a group of ten or twelve kindred souls to meet each Friday, for such was the original plan. The host would outline the subject for debate, and this was to be followed by limited period for rejoinder. The exact time for rejoinder was never specified, but by common consent was not to exceed five minutes.

At the initial meeting represented was John Blair, of the State School Planning Board. For law there was Currin Keeble and Mr. Brown Shepherd, another attorney. Our own Dr. Hubert Royster was for medicine, and of course not to be forgotten was Dr. Clarence Shore, of the State Laboratory of Hygiene. Mr. Ted Johnson was an engineer, Mr. Harrison Panton, another one. The cloth was represented by Rev. Mr. Way, Principal of St. Mary's School, whose opposite number today is Dr. Campbell of Meredith College, and Mr. Jack Ellis, at that time incumbent at the Pullen Memorial Church.

With certain exceptions, this was supposed to represent a cross section of the available intelligentsia of Raleigh. If it was supposed that each member would be limited to his field and so provide a rounded program for the year, the idea was completely repudiated by the Club membership. They decided to talk upon the subject which appealed to each the most and more often than not this was without his chosen field. The grass always grows greener you know. "A man's a man for a' that" and represents restraint, so it was concluded to each speaker enough rope to hang himself with.

We have one member who could hang the lot of us and never leave his field. I refer to Dr. Raymond Murray of Nuclear Engineering.

It is an old story now, but Dr. Hamilton will bear me out that with all the ropings and hangings there has never been a known case of a Sandwicher who left a meeting with a changed opinion, a compliment to the firmness of the minds of the members.

With the Sandwich Club fairly launched upon its way it was soon seen that the character of its leader, Captain Sam Lawrence, was initially and subsequently responsible for its success. I suppose that few gentler characters ever lived in Raleigh, but for purpose of discipline he successfully concealed the fact with a droll humor, so that he became known as the Mussolini of the Sandwich Club. Woe unto the man who allowed other engagement to come before attendance. He was hastened in irons to the dungeon. However his good natured tyranny was never resented.

Certain things were accomplished under his leadership. The time for meetings was set for every other Friday. I think there must have been protest from the lady members. The fiction of the Sandwich Dinner of cracker-box crackers and coca-cola was done away with when it was proven that the empty vessel makes the most noise. And Ladies Night was established to be held upon the date nearest the anniversary of that other great devotee to Truth, George Washington. This date coincided with the founding of the Sandwich Club.

We know that it is not always the browbeating personality who exercises the greatest force for leadership. It is more often the man like Captain Sam whose touch was as light as his spirit gentle. When I speak of him it comes back to me that indeed I lost a true friend. All honor to his authority. If he had his choice, I am sure that his monument would not stand in the public square, nor yet upon the silent hill. He would have it remain, where it is today, in the hearts of his friends.

Captain Sam's mantle fell upon the shoulders of Judge George W. Connor, one of the later members but none the less beloved. First of all he had been a practicing attorney, afterward a circuit judge, and finally a judge of the highest court of his State. What better qualification for leadership could he have had?

Judge Michael Schenck, a colleague of the Bench, was an excellent member. The fact that his manner was subdued did not indicate a lack of humor. The following story of the Judge's will show.

General Kilpatrick, Sherman's former Chief of Cavalry, was appointed to command of North Carolina after the war was over, with headquarters at Salisbury. It was sometime later that he published in the

Philadelphia Public Ledger the following story.

"When I was in command of the State of North Carolina after the end of hostilities, I had the pleasure of placing Governor Vance in arrest and forcing him to ride the twenty-eight miles to headquarters on the back of a mule."

Little did the General know the quality of the quarry he had aroused. Governor Vance immediately asked the paper for privilege of reply. This is the answer of the Governor.

"It is true that, while I was a guest at the home of a friend near Hickory I received a call from a very courteous officer of the Union Army, who stated that it was his duty to place me in arrest."

"My friend placed his horse and buggy at our disposal and drove to Salisbury. Upon the way I do not recall having seen a mule. But, when we neared the post of command at Salisbury, I thought I distinguished the braying of an ass. Which impression has since been confirmed."

There is no record of further comment from General Kilpatrick.

Here is a story of the Judge's home town, Greensboro, where lived another jurist famed for his knowledge of the law but completely devoid of a sense of humor.

One morning in Judge Dick's court, the Plaintiff's attorney arose to say that his client and principal witness, Miss Sarah Mooney, was confined to bed and unable to be present. So he asked for continuance. The attorney for the defense promptly arose to say that he did not object to the request, since it would be entirely wrong to proceed without ceremony.

There was a titter and laughter in the courtroom. Judge Dick rapped sternly for order and continued the case.

It was not until the dinner hour that Mrs. Dick observed the judge holding to the gate post apparently convulsed in laughter.

"Judge Dick come in here at once to your dinner. What on earth is the matter?"

"My dear, the funniest thing happened in court this morning." Then he related the story using the name Mary Mooney instead of Sarah Mooney.

"Why, Judge Dick," said his wife. "I don't see anything to laugh at in that."

"Well, my dear, I didn't at first, but it will come to you."

Currin Keeble betrayed no affection for the law for which he had been educated. Beside this, he had held post as instructor in literature at State College. Ah here was the profession which lay close to his heart, and in this field he was supreme. His masterpiece, a talk entitled, THE LITERATURE OF SATIRE, I was not privileged to hear, yet to say that it was Currin's masterpiece was praise enough. He was a very close friend of mine and I miss him every day.

One of our attorneys, Willis Briggs, scored a splendid triumph, which in the annals of the Sandwich Club has never been surpassed.

Dr. J. B. Rhine of Duke, famed for his discoveries in extrasensory perception, had been invited to the Club on condition that he bring his cards, which you understand are to be identified when viewed from the back. In order to make the test more complete, the deck to be used was unknown even to Dr. Rhine.

Now when the plan became known to the wife of the host-to-be, she eagerly agreed to furnish an equal number of feminine contestants. So, the contest was not limited to the Sandwich Club but took on the proportions of contest between male and female.

So often had the male members heard, from the ladies of course, of female intuition, there was considerable trepidation lest the men be not able to hold their ground.

Dr. Rhine announced that the answer would be determined by statistics of which even he was ignorant. Well for the score, every single man triumphed over his female opponent, and, when it came to finding out who among the men had the highest score, it was found that it was Willis Briggs who had outclassed all the lawyers and doctors and what have you.

Among the lawyers, I should speak of Mr. I. M. Bailey, who did much in Utilities and of Mr. Ruark; both of these attorneys were of the highest standard at the Raleigh Bar. I should speak also of Mr. Brown Shepherd, and of Mr. Francis Paschal, who was with us but a short time before his ability was recognized and he was called to the faculty at Duke.

As for physicians, our own Dr. Hubert Royster never needed introduction to a North Carolina audience. Up until the time he was in his eighties, his mind was as active as his body. He had been an athlete in his youth, and in fact he served as referee for football games when he was past sixty-five. Dr. Royster never lost his interest in contest.

I suppose that no finer character nor a kinder man ever lived in North Carolina than Dr. C. A. Shore. He was a gentleman in every meaning of the term. But, should anyone suppose that he lacked strength of conviction, just let him try to change Clarence Shore where a matter of principle was involved. I think that no one ever succeeded in that. His untimely death was one of the greatest losses North Carolina ever sustained.

Another physician upon the roster of the Sandwich Club was Dr. V. M. Hicks and that brings us to the present time when we have Chauncey Royster and Alfred Hamilton.

While we are medically minded, I ask your permission to relate an incident which occurred at home.

I was interested in the human brain and I thought the Club would find research interesting. So over to Chapel Hill I went and was fortunate in securing the assistance of one of their specialists.

A little after six the physician arrived carrying two buckets in either hand.

"What do you have there?" I cried in dismay.

"Well you told me you wanted brains, so I brought some along."

Early in the evening he took the lids from his buckets and there upon my wife's piano top exposed four pieces of human machinery. Nothing to indicate whether the original possessor had been a criminal or a philanthropist, they lay there in silent tribute to the master work of the Master Mind.

It seemed remarkable that we could sit there and have pointed out to us the visual area, and others, smell, hearing, touch, etc. It seemed hard to realize that this machine, more complicated than all the machines man has made and put together, could have been the directing force of a human being not long deceased. But so it was.

And then some member described to the doctor the triumph of Willis Briggs, and asked him to point out the area responsible for this feat.

The doctor appeared uninterested. He either wouldn't or couldn't.

N. C. State College has been a rich source for new members. Dr. Wells, a plant biologist, we had until he moved out of town and out of range of our meetings. Frank Rice, formerly of the Chemistry Dept., was a charming member until a good promotion lured him away. Today we have Addison Hickman, Ralph Fadum, something of a world traveler, and Dr. Ray Murray.

The latter holds position in the field of Nuclear Energy, a fascinating subject and almost impossible for the layman.

Now we are used to thinking of submarines driven by nuclear power; but Ray is my authority for saying that nuclear power may be eclipsed by fusion power. I say may advisedly for there is no present substance which can control fusion when confined. But, consider that the energy which could be derived from a teaspoon of water would be capable of driving a passenger train from London to Glasgow and return.

At the present time, our submarines can go around the world without having to stop for refueling. We are living in an age of miracles, it is easy to see compared to conditions obtaining when I was young. Nuclear plants are being built now. If they are built they will be used. It will not be too much to say that the entire power picture will be changed, at least for some countries.

This gives me the opportunity to introduce a miracle brain. Cornelius Brennecke was as brilliant a man as it has ever been my privilege to know. I treasure each hour of my association with him.

Dr. Brennecke is listed in "Who's Who" and again in a companion work, "Who's Who in Engineering." The list of his achievements recited there since his graduation at Columbia University is too long to quote. He was head of the Department of Electrical Engineering at State.

Outside of his profession, he was a man of a variety of attainments. He was a competent musician as well as a musical critic, a performer on both the piano and organ. I recall a delightful evening at his home, when he entertained us with his stereophonic equipment, emphasizing the selections with his comments. He was a keen judge of literature which was worthwhile. He had no patience with shoddy work. This last was characteristic of the man in all of his activities.

Speaking for myself, when Cornelius Brennecke passed at an all too early age, something went out of my life. I always felt free to consult him. I recall one evening, after I had been bold enough to take on the subject of television, I found myself in trouble and it was Dr. Brennecke who straightened me out. He was generous of his talent.

I should speak of Dr. Clarence Poe, a good business man and a very successful publisher. We now have Sam Ragan to represent him and in direct line Mr. Chas. Poe.

I shall speak now of one whose interest in literature rivals his love for politics. It is my pleasure since I am a profound admirer of his literary technique, though by nature I cannot follow the achievement in politics of Mr. Edwin Gill. I shall cite his latest talk which will furnish an example.

Mr. Gill carried us back to an important date in history 135 years ago. A group had assembled at Monticello. Present were Thomas Jefferson, The Marquis de Lafayette, James Madison, and James Monroe.

The whole thing turned out to be fantasy. There was no stenographic report so Mr. Gill made his own.

The freedom of the press had been recognized for only one year. This led to reference to Thomas Paine.

The talk around the dinner table gave an analysis of the political ancestry of our nation. Jefferson faced challenge as to why he had not in his term of office opposed slavery more strongly than he did, since his personal opposition was known. Jefferson replied that the time for such action was premature. It is a fact, I believe, that at his death Jefferson freed his own slaves.

With all, it was a most interesting review of the political genesis of our ideas. I do not believe that there is another man in North Carolina who could have done it as well as Mr. Gill.

As for the Gentlemen of the Cloth, we now have Gaylord Noyce, a man who lives his faith.

I have heard it said that, though the specialist has his field, it is the business man who must face a variety of issues and decide quickly. Upon the way these issues are decided will often depend the success of his company.

This is certainly true of the banking business. We have had among our members one of the leaders of one of the South's largest banks. To his fine business judgment, Mr. [George] Geoghegan adds a charming and understanding manner, which has qualified him for the position of Public Relations Officer, a position which he has filled with marked success.

Another Sandwich member who has demonstrated his business ability is Hal Trentman. Almost from the beginning he has met and successfully solved the many problems for a business lately moved to new territory. He has brought his company to a position which would entitle it to be acclaimed with pride by any city of the South.

In addition to the work which he has done for his company, he has been allied with a number of civic enterprises of which the airport will serve as an example. And he has endeared himself to a host of friends.

I must acknowledge my personal indebtedness to Mr. Zack Arthur. With a battery of stenographers at his disposal he has been so generous as to take the burden of detail from my shoulders.

Mr. Arthur's ability has now been recognized, and he has become the head of the Great American Insurance Company for their operations in North Carolina, South Carolina, and Virginia, a promotion of which any insurance man might be proud.

I like to think that the friendly spirit of Captain Sam Lawrence still looks down upon the institution which he had loved so well.

1924 to 1960 is a period of thirty-six years, a goodly portion of a man's lifetime, but it seems to me that the spirit of the Club has not diminished but on the contrary grown stronger. It has been to me not only a major interest in life but a predominant one. I have come to count living in good measure by the time between meetings.

For despite the fact that my convictions may not have been changed, I have information which has come to me from the lips of my friends. For that reason it is the more highly prized.

I like to think too of our genial Judge Connor. He came to the Club late in life but his interest was none the less keen. It seems to me that with two such spirits to guide us as Captain Sam and Judge Connor, it will be hard to turn us back.

The Sandwich Club was founded upon sound principle. There are not too many members so that everybody has his say without unduly prolonging the evening. Also a tightly knit group is strong for friendship.

For the thing which has held our club together is friendship, which when reciprocated, comes close to love, the master cement of the Universe.

I thank you.

"Here They Are" Poems

Discovered in the files of the Sandwich Club is an unusual set of poems about the members. We will never know who the author or authors were, but surely members did not write their own poems. We suspect that the chairman assigned the poem writing. Because the styles of the poems vary so greatly (the entry for Michael Schenck is not even a poem), we think it is possible that each member was assigned a poem about another member. We include the literature just as it was written, for the reader's amusement.

▣ ▣ ▣

HERE THEY ARE
Author Unknown

SANDWICH CLUB
Ladies' Night
Colonial Pines Hotel
February 23, 1945

I. M. Bailey

'Tis said his clients never blush;
For Rotary Clubs he has a crush.
On foreign affairs he will not hush –
He's seldom quiet.
The ladies know his eyes are brown;
He's one of the tallest men in town.
I'll bet you've never seen him frown –
Oh, he's a riot.

M. V. Barnhill

He's versed in things juridical,
And eke affairs political;
In history he's quite a star,
And comfortable at a bar.

14

His speech betrays not his vocation
('Tis not black market operation);
Ne'er once in all his life I'll say
Has he confronted O. P. A.

In body spare, but not in mind;
Indeed in no club can you find
A man in reasoning more profound
Or one who's surer of his ground.

Willis Briggs

White is mingled in his hair
Independence is his air
Lean, but not long,
Lawyer to right wrong.
Inches eight, feet five,
Scribe – very much alive.

Bright of eye, sound of mind.
Right ahead, not behind.
In his knowledge of the town,
Gives us stories as if wound.
Good of looks, old of name
Say, my friends, he's very tame.

Carlyle Campbell

Endowed with grace
He knows his place
In matters great and small.
If you're in doubt
Just call him out
He answers every call.

He likes to walk
He loves to talk
He's always up to date.
He spends his days
In finding ways
His ideas to state.

It is no joke
He loves to smoke

A nice big fat cigar.
He teaches girls
With golden curls
Who come from near and far.

George Geoghegan   He is suave and very swank
So the ladies give him rank,
Say he's tops, and I'm frank
I do too. He runs the bank.

Chas. E. Johnson   Though we say he's a "Benito,"
    still no one would call him "lini"
It's the table he reduces.
Then with pencil he produces
Seeming order out of chaos and a likeness
    of your "beany."

With his chores performed, though
    prophets rage, in pace requiescit
From alarms and plagues defended.
His serenity amended,
He again becomes our fuehrer – great in
    mind and heart and weskit.

Theo. S. Johnson   His name stands for judging why heads
    not so small
Can hold all he knows and so clearly recall.
He's always so genial – and this is a virtue –
It's not hard to tell which views he will nurture.
His face and his figure so seldom perversed
Will cause you to think of the thin man reversed.
His jobs are quite various and, in truth to tell,
He does them with vigor and ever so well.
We wonder what gives him such perfect relief,
Whether preacher or lawyer, merchant or chief,
Vocation, profession or public concern –
In whatever sequence his talents may turn.
Of course, he's "outstanding," I'm glad to reveal;
His other endowments I perforce conceal.

C. G. Keeble

There once was a man, Currin Keeble,
As a defender of arts, far from feeble.
For old Greece he votes yes;
Of the British, much less;
And of war's end, just a guess.

Hubert A. Royster

A lifelong cut-up. Master of blades.
Ectomic specialist. To the very last
Eliminator of the naughty protoplast,
Forgetting never the sponges on these raids.
Hero in white of knifely escapades,
He moves undaunted, nor aghast
In psychic worlds of present and of past.
And nothing on those journeys, he evades.
Returning, this restless, sapient mind
Will compare worlds, but you take care,
Since he to Sandwich friends has often spoke
The slaying formula of an ancient kind
Which he will drag from Cicero's lair
And get you with his "Post hoc ergo propter hoc."

Robert Ruark

He's poker-faced, dignified, deliberate in action.
Of bulldog tenacity he has more than fraction.
New Deal ideology and regimentation
Will never receive the least commendation
From this able member, highly respected,
Whose name, ere now, you will have detected.

Michael Schenck

The subject of this sketch is a well known character about town. His height is above the average. His weight perhaps somewhat under the average. He is a brunette. He does not curl his hair. He moves with deliberation, but takes very short steps considering the length of his bipeds.

He frequently expresses his views upon matters of greater or less interest, sometimes to particular individuals only, and sometimes to numerous persons of varied opinions. Frequently his statements are difficult of interpretation even by trained minds. Frequently and from time to time his expressed views are considered as clearly wrong. That they are so considered does not seem to disturb him. No one doubts his integrity. He has been known to publicly change his previously entertained and publicly expressed views, but not often. How often he may have changed his privately entertained and expressed views cannot be approximated, but, being married, it is fair to assume frequently.

His outward bearing tends to be solemn but he has been known on occasion to actually laugh at a good joke.

In spite of what has been said, he measures up to the most exacting definition of "Gentleman."

W. H. Trentman

Sanguine, facile, suave and bland
At promotion, quite a hand.
Egregious, yes, but ego small.
Introversive – not at all!
Countenance and stature, handsome
In fact I'd say he's quite a man, mum!

B. W. Wells

Chaos rioted through endless space
Till Integration moved forth apace.
Differentiation made poor Adam an ape.
And Satan created his tricky mate.
Epigenetic organicism now vainly produce,
The sperm and amoeba have grown obtuse.
Calamitous fate has puny man on the bend
And all our wars and glories at an end.
Dire oblivion soon on us most fall
On thee, on me, indeed, my friends, on all.

Comments by Raymond L. Murray

For more than 50 years I have been grateful for the opportunity to be a member of the Sandwich Club. It has provided intellectual stimulation for me throughout my later life, through the challenge of preparing presentations, and hearing papers and comments from others. It has been a source of different ideas and information. I have been pleased to be able to learn from members with a variety of backgrounds and talents. Finally, it facilitated warm and lasting friendships based on common interests.

There is an ancient precedent for a dinner discussion group, Samuel Johnson's "The Club." This organization was founded nearly 250 years ago, in February 1764, by Johnson and the artist Joshua Reynolds. Among the members were the statesman Edmund Burke, Johnson's biographer James Boswell, economist Adam Smith, and author Edward Gibbon. The Club was in existence as late as 1911. Winston Churchill wanted to join, but was considered too controversial, so in 1911 he founded "The Other Club" and became its chairman. This new group had 12 rules which were read aloud each meeting. Churchill brought in Aristotle Onassis, to the surprise of other members.

As noted earlier, we know that the name of our organization was based on the simple meals served by the early club members. But we are also familiar with the origin of the word "sandwich." Quoting from a newspaper article, "...the fourth Earl of Sandwich was first lord of the admiralty and he financed the expedition of Captain Cook, who kindly named the Sandwich Islands after him (later they became Hawaii). He was also a bon vivant whose eureka moment, legend has it, came during an all-night gambling session, when, rather than waste time by sitting down to dinner, he ate a hunk of meat between two pieces of bread and gambled on." Perhaps the early Sandwich Club members felt an affinity for the Earl of Sandwich and his eureka moment.

The papers by club members over the years have been of excellent quality, as the result of extensive research and preparation.

As of this writing, the old section of the North Carolina Museum of Art has re-opened, with a Norman Rockwell exhibit. This reminds me about the story of the acquisition of the major collection of paintings. One of our former members, Edwin Gill, was instrumental in purchasing artwork worth a million dollars in New York City, using a grant from the North Carolina General Assembly. Sadly, his role in augmenting the art collection does not show up in the North Carolina Department of State

Treasurer website or the history of NCMA, or any other sources that could be found.

Edwin gave a paper on his accomplishment to a Sandwich Club Ladies Night on February 14, 1958.

I can mention some amusing incidents. In the comment period of many meetings, one of our members rambled on for what seemed like hours. Consequently, we initiated a five-minute rule for comments. Recently, we discovered that the same time interval had been agreed on by the founders of the club.

On one occasion, a member had prepared his comments in advance when he heard the topic of the next presentation was to be on "whales." When he arrived at the meeting, he quickly discovered that the correct topic was "Wales." His misunderstanding was the subject of much amusement.

Raleigh's Sandwich Club and its history is not well known, but it did receive an interesting mention in a recent publication. Emily Wilson's book consists of letters between Elizabeth Lawrence and a playwright friend. There is a footnote reading, "Elizabeth's father, Sam Lawrence, founded the Sandwich Club for men in Raleigh in 1924. The members met once a month in one another's homes to read their original philosophic papers." The Greensboro newspaper *News & Record* that reviewed the book ended by saying, "This is a nice book. But I still would like to know more about that Sandwich Club. Philosophers in Raleigh?" Yes, indeed.

And I'm proud to have been part of this unique brotherhood for the past 50-plus years. -- RLM

Comments by H. G. Jones

Dr. H. G. Jones was a member for more than 40 years, from 1968 to 2010. During that period he visited Alaska and Canada frequently. He made friends with the Inuits and collected their artwork. Several of his papers dealt with his experiences in the far North.

We asked H. G. for some thoughts on and memories of his history as a member of the Sandwich Club:

One of my most vivid memories is State Treasurer Edwin Gill's obsession with North Carolina's No. 1 national credit rating. Nearly all of his papers (and often his comments on the papers of others) included a reminder of the accomplishment that of course was largely due to the frugality with which he handled North Carolina's finances.

Among the genuine intellectuals was Dr. Jacob Koomen, whose papers on rather mundane interesting subjects (for example, "corn" and "mustard") became learned discussions with all sorts of interesting twists and turns.

I was impressed too, by the intellectual curiosity of physicians Alfred Hamilton and Chauncey Royster, whose papers could also be thought-provoking.

During public controversies over the disposition of hazardous materials, Chairman Raymond Murray was one of the few academicians who understood the implications and who counseled public leaders, some of whom yielded to political rather than scientific influence.

During my career, I resisted joining other civic clubs and discussion groups to which I would not have time to give full attention. So the Sandwich Club is the only one whose invitation I accepted. It was a wise decision, and I am grateful for having been given the opportunity to associate with fellow members over the years. -- HGJ

Sandwich Club in 1971

STANDING: John V. Hunter III, H.G. Jones, Chauncey L. Royster, James S. Currie, Edward L. Rankin Jr., William H. Sprunt III, and Charles A. Poe. SEATED: Ralph B. Reeves Jr., Raymond L. Murray, T. Harry Gatton, Alfred Hamilton, Edwin Gill, Charles D. Arthur, Harlan E. Boyles, and Jacob Koomen, Jr. Photo was taken by Burnie Batchelor in a private room in the lower level of Balentine's Cafeteria in Cameron Village.

Sandwich Club in 2001

STANDING: James E. Stewart, Thomas J. Harrelson, John C. Martin, J. Parker Chesson, Jr., John B. Lewis, Jr., and W. Kern Holoman. SEATED: Fred R. DeJarnette, A. G. Bullard, Jr., Raymond L. Murray, H. G. Jones, Jacob Koomen, Jr., and J. Allen Norris, Jr. Not pictured: Thomas H. Campbell, Garrett Briggs, and Thomas H. McGuire, Jr. Photo was taken by the Burnie Batchelor Studio in a private room in the Carolina Country Club.

Sandwich Club Roster

Member	From	To
Lawrence, Samuel	1924	-
Johnson, Charles	1924	1962
Royster, Hubert	1924	1957
Wells, B. W.	1924	1958
Strange, J. V.	1924	-
Seagle, P. E.	1924	-
Poe, Clarence	1924	-
Hicks, V. M.	1924	-
Way, Rev. W. W.	1924	-
Ellis, Jack	1924	-
Shepherd, Brown	1924	-
Shore, Clarence	1924	-
Blair, John	1924	-
Johnson, Ted	1924	-
Keeble, Currin	1924	-
Ruark, Robert, Sr. *	1924	-
Panton, Harrison	-	-
Connor, George	-	-
Schenck, Michael	-	-
Briggs, Willis	-	-
Bailey, I. M.	-	-
Paschal, Francis	-	-
Brennecke, Cornelius	-	-
Hickman, Addison	-	1960
Gill, Edwin	-	1979

* Robert Ruark's family explains that he never used the "Senior" suffix, but we insert it here because our earliest membership rosters list him in such a way.

Geoghegan, George	-	1967
Campbell, Carlyle	-	1967
Poe, Charles	-	1991
Fadum, Ralph	-	1966
Trentman, Hal	-	1978
Royster, Chauncey	-	1990
Arthur, Charles	-	1992
Murray, Raymond	1957	
Hamilton, Alfred	1958	1979
Noyce, Gaylord	1958	1960
Ragan, Sam	1958	1969
Andrews, Alex	1961	1964
Currie, James	1962	1991
Gatton, Harry	1963	2001
Sprunt, William	1965	1973
Bailey, Ruffin	1966	1967
Rankin, Edward	1967	1972
Koomen, Jacob	1968	2005
Reeves, Ralph	1968	1984
Jones, H. G.	1968	2009
Hunter, John	1968	1977
	1990	1997
Browne, Micou	1969	1971
Boyles, Harlan	1969	1997
Parker, Frank	1971	1981
Wilson, William	1975	1989
Caldwell, John	1977	1978
Wishy, Bernard	1977	1983
Johnson, Harvey	1979	1991
Royster, Henry	1980	1999
Patterson, A. M.	1981	1990
Menius, A. C.	1984	1997

Speidel, George	1984	1994
Holoman, Kern	1984	
London, George	1985	1993
Briggs, Garrett	1991	2006
Campbell, Thomas	1992	2004
Moss, Arthur	1992	1998
Lewis, John	1992	
Bullard, A. G.	1993	2008
Norris, Allen	1993	2004
Deane, Tenney	1993	1996
Park, Ben	1994	1998
DeJarnette, Fred	1996	
Martin, John	1997	
Chesson, Parker	1997	2009
McGuire, Thomas	1997	2003
Stewart, James	1998	
McNutt, James	1998	1999
Barnhardt, Robert	2001	
Long, Ray	2001	2005
Harrelson, Thomas	2001	2009
Struik, Hendrik	2005	
Jenkins, Bill	2007	2009
Donald Weisenborn	2007	
Grady, Perry	2007	
Finkelstein, Zane	2011	

- Indicates where records are incomplete and dates are unknown.

Biographies of Members

A decision was made to try to present biographical sketches of all past and present members. These vary in length, depending on availability of information. Current and recent members were asked to compose their own material, giving as a minimum birthdate and place, education, family, career history with principal accomplishments, and interesting experiences and events.

Very little information was preserved from the earliest days of the Sandwich Club. Sometimes we had only a name and a date of a member's tenure; sometimes not even a complete date; and sometimes only first initials and not full names. As a result, with many members, our research had to start with square one.

For some members, the information came from the text submitted by a prospective member's sponsor. The *Dictionary of North Carolina Biography*, edited by William Powell, was the source of several sketches. Raleigh City Directories were invaluable. A few bios were found on the Internet. Prominent there were Clarence Poe, Sam Ragan, and Edwin Gill. University publications, professional journals and promotional materials about local businesses were helpful. The Olivia Raney Local History Library was able to supply several obituaries as they appeared in the Raleigh *News & Observer*. Family members also provided much needed material for some of the Sandwich Club members.

For early members the North Carolina Collection at the University of North Carolina at Chapel Hill was an excellent source. It included newspaper articles about individuals, the *News & Observer*'s "Tar Heel of the Week" features, and obituaries.

The search for sketches was greatly facilitated by the help of Dr. H. G. Jones, former head of the North Carolina Collection and until recently a member of the Sandwich Club. Dr. Jones made the original suggestion that a history of the club should be written, and made a number of valuable suggestions.

It was decided not to edit the texts of the biographical material unless some of the information was irrelevant. Thus, the amount of space devoted to members varies greatly and the text reflects the time it was written. Rather than change a great deal, we preserved that point of view and the tone of the original text. Therefore readers will experience sketches in both third and first person, past and present tense, and texts with obvious original purposes, like obituaries.

We encourage readers who have additional information on Sandwich Club members to share what they know with the club's historian. Preserving the club's history, and therefore information on its members, is an on-going project.

Finally, we made every effort to identity the former members with as much accuracy as possible. This was not always easy. Some names are common. Some names are shared by other more famous individuals. For example, Sandwich Club member Robert Ruark was hard to track down because of frequent references to a different Robert Ruark, who happened to be the father of the famous journalist, adventurer, and author Robert Ruark, Jr.

It was important to us that we find as much as possible about the lives of the members, not just names, places and dates. The Sandwich Club has been and continues to be comprised of individuals who bring with them unique experiences and perspectives. It is the sum of these varied experiences that makes the Sandwich Club the vibrant, ever-changing entity that it is. Therefore, the knowledge and preservation of the individual members and the complexities of their lives is essential to understanding the history of the Sandwich Club of Raleigh as a whole.

The members and their biographies are listed in the order in which they appear on the roster.

SAMUEL LAWRENCE

Samuel Lawrence was born in 1874, the son of Robert de Treville Lawrence and Ann Eliza Atkinson Lawrence of Marietta, Georgia. He graduated from the University of Georgia.

Mr. Lawrence became a resident of Raleigh in 1916, when he came here from Hamlet to become a member of the firm of Lawrence Stone and Gravel Company. For several years before then he had been connected with W. R. Bonsal and Company, paving contractors of Hamlet. For a number of years he served as division engineer for the Seaboard Air Line Railway.

A member of the Christ Church Vestry, Lawrence was one of the leading laymen of the Episcopal Church in North Carolina. In 1924 he helped to found the Sandwich Club, a men's forum club, and served as chairman of the organization from its beginning until his death.

His daughter Elizabeth was a Raleigh landscape designer, an author of three classic books. A description of her garden in Charlotte appears in an Internet website report by Davyd Foard Hood.

As noted in the 1960 paper by Charles Johnson, early in February 1924 Captain Sam Lawrence "breezed" into his office with a proposition. His idea was to assemble a group of ten or twelve kindred souls to meet every Friday for a dinner and discussion. Sam Lawrence can thus be credited with the origin of the Sandwich Club.

Sam Lawrence died July 16, 1936, at his home 115 Park Avenue in Raleigh.

He was survived by his wife, who before marriage was Miss Elizabeth Bardenbaugh of Parkersburg, West Virginia; two daughters, Miss Elizabeth Lewis Lawrence of Raleigh and Miss Ann de Treville Lawrence of New York; two brothers, the Rev. James Bolan Lawrence of Americus, Georgia, and Marion McDonald Lawrence of Marietta, Georgia; and a sister-in-law, Mrs. Alexander Atkinson Lawrence of Savannah, Georgia.[1]

---

[1] Adapted from obituary, *News and Observer*, Raleigh, North Carolina, July 17, 1936, courtesy of Olivia Raney Local History Library, Raleigh, North Carolina; www.winghavengardens.com accessed 7 January 2011; Elizabeth Lawrence website www.elizabethlawrence.org accessed 7 June 2010.

CHARLES JOHNSON

Charles Johnson was a charter member and co-organizer of the Sandwich Club. He was both an insurance man and a historian. He died in 1962 at his home 1701-A McDonald Lane at the age of 78.

Mr. Johnson was organizer of the Charles E. Johnson and Sons insurance agency, from which he retired in 1960 after a half century with the firm.

He was also president of the Hamlet Ice Company and for many years was treasurer of the Atlantic Fire Insurance Company, which was organized in Raleigh. He was engaged in banking earlier in his career.

He was born in Raleigh on September 22, 1883, the son of Charles Earl Johnson and Mrs. Mary Wilson Johnson. He was educated at the Morson-Denson School here, and graduated from the University of North Carolina in 1903. During World War I, he served as an infantry lieutenant in France and later was the first commander of American Legion Post No. 1 here. As noted he was a member of the Sandwich Club, a literary organization. He was a former president of the Carolina Country Club.

Until shortly before his death, he lived at 120 Hillsboro Street. He interested himself in the history of Raleigh and wrote a series of newspaper articles about old Raleigh.

He was survived by his wife, Mrs. Nancy White Johnson; four sons, the Rev. Charles E. Johnson, Jr. of Duke University, Durham, and Bradford W. Johnson, Richard M. Johnson and Harvey W. Johnson, all of Raleigh; and 13 grandchildren.

Funeral services were held at Christ Church, conducted by the Rev. A. Moody Burt, assisted by the Rev. James McDowell Dick. Charles Johnson was buried in Oakwood Cemetery.[2]

DR. HUBERT A. ROYSTER

Dr. Hubert Ashley Royster, pioneer North Carolina surgeon, died in Raleigh in November 1962 at the age of 87.

Dr. Royster was the first physician in the State to specialize in surgery,

---

[2] Adapted from obituary, *News and Observer*, Raleigh, North Carolina, July 2, 1962. Courtesy of North Carolina Collection, University of North Carolina, Chapel Hill, North Carolina.

beginning in 1906.

He was a Raleigh native, and after medical training, returned here in 1896 to enter practice with his father, Dr. W. I. Royster. Five years later he married Miss Louise Page of Maryland. He resided at 2318 Beechridge Road.

With Honors

In 1891, he was graduated with honors from Wake Forest College, and took his medical degree from the University of Pennsylvania in 1894. He served his internship at Mercy Hospital, Pittsburgh, Pa., the following year.

From 1902-1910 he was dean of the University of North Carolina Medical School, then located in Raleigh. At the time of his death he was Professor of Surgery, Emeritus, of the University's School of Medicine in Chapel Hill.

In association with officials of St. Augustine's College he founded St. Agnes Hospital, and became chief of surgery for that Negro institution. Until his retirement in 1939 he was also chief of surgery of Rex Hospital and consulting surgeon to the State Hospital here.

He was president of the Wake County Medical Society in 1912 and the North Carolina Medical Society in 1922. He was one of the founders and a fellow of the American College of Surgeons and a member of the American Surgical Association. For many years, he was secretary of the Southern Surgical Association and its president in 1926. At his retirement he was professor of surgery at Wake Forest College.

He was author of *Syllabus of Therapeutics* (1899), *Textbook on Appendicitis* (1927), and *Medical Morals & Manners* (1937). He wrote extensively for medical journals, and was on the editorial board of the *N.C. Medical Journal*.

In World War I he served as a medical member of the Advisory Committee of the Council of National Defense.

Surviving him besides his wife were two sons, Dr. Hubert A. Royster Jr., of Bryn Mawr, Pa.; Dr. Henry P. Royster of Philadelphia; one daughter, Mrs. Virginia Page Oxnard of Savannah, Ga.; and a nephew, Dr. Chauncey L. Royster of Raleigh.[3]

---

[3] Adapted from obituary, *News and Observer*, Raleigh, North Carolina, November 19, 1962. Courtesy of North Carolina Collection, University of North Carolina, Chapel Hill, North Carolina.

DR. B. W. WELLS

Dr. Bertram Whittier Wells, former head of the botany department at N.C. State University, died in December 1978. He was 94.

Wells, of Route 1, Wake Forest, headed the botany department from 1919 to 1949 and retired from teaching in 1954.

Although he regarded teaching as his major contribution, Wells was known throughout the state for the hundreds of field trips he made.

Wells was born in Troy, Ohio, on March 5, 1884. After receiving his doctorate from the University of Chicago in 1917, he taught at Knox College in Galesburg, Ill., at Connecticut Agricultural College and at Kansas State Agricultural College. He was head of the botany department at the University of Arkansas in 1918-1919.

Dr. Stephen G. Boyce, chief forest ecologist for the U.S. Forest Service in Asheville, said he had traveled to the coast with Wells for two summers in the early 1950s to do research for a doctoral dissertation.

"We'd sit on the beach and talk about everything from geology to politics," Boyce said in a telephone interview.

Dr. Wells, an Ohio native, was a Tar Heel of the Week in January 1955. In that interview with the *News and Observer*, he said one of his major discoveries was his finding that the action of salt rather than the action of the wind determined the shape of coastal vegetation.

Boyce said that after Dr. Wells had seen aerial photographs made by the government of the coastal area in the 1930s, he postulated that the Carolina Bays were formed by meteorite showers hundreds of thousands of years ago.

"He presented that theory to the North Carolina Academy of Sciences in the early forties ... and to my knowledge it's never really been disproven," Boyce said.

Wells, who lived on a farm in northern Wake County, was author of *The Natural Gardens of North Carolina*, a book published in 1932 by the University Press.

After retiring at the age of 70, Wells lived and worked on his 150-acre farm in northern Wake County.

He was survived by his wife, Maude Barnes Wells.[4]

---

[4] Adapted from obituary, *News and Observer*, Raleigh, North Carolina, December 30, 1978. Courtesy of North Carolina Collection, University of North Carolina, Chapel Hill, North Carolina.

J. V. STRANGE

J. V. Strange was one of the founding members of the Sandwich Club in 1924.

John Vanderveet Strange was born on September 29, 1882, in King City, Missouri. He attended the Portland Academy in Portland, Oregon, and graduated from there on October 12, 1909.

Strange remained in Portland where he worked with the Pacific Power and Light Company in the early 1920s. By 1921, he was listed as Chairman of that electric company.

It is thought that J. V. Strange moved to Raleigh sometime around 1924, when he became a founding member of the Sandwich Club. He joined the staff of the Carolina Power and Light Company, and became the Vice-President/Operating Manager by 1930.

J. V. Strange and his wife Mary M. Strange lived at 925 Holt Drive in the Hayes-Barton neighborhood. They had two sons, John M. and Robert F. Strange, who were listed as students living with their parents in the *1930 Raleigh City Directory*.[5]

PERRY SEAGLE

Perry Edgar Seagle was born in 1883 in Hendersonville. He was the son of Philip Seagle and Mary Drake Seagle. He graduated from the University of North Carolina at Chapel Hill, where he was selected as a member of Phi Beta Kappa in 1906. He played on the varsity football team during his four years of college.

Perry taught at Oak Ridge Military Academy and served as principal of Murphey School in Raleigh and of Wilmington High School. He then became the North Carolina representative for Ginn and Company, publishers of textbooks and other educational materials. He was manager of the local office at 20 East Martin Street.

Seagle was a senior warden of Christ Episcopal Church in Raleigh. He was mentioned in the *Journal of the Annual Convention of the Protestant Episcopal Church in North Carolina*. The meeting was held May 17-19, 1911.

---

[5] *Raleigh City Directory, 1930;* Strange, Alexander Taylor, *Biographical and Historical Sketches of the Stranges of America and Across the Sea*, 1911.

Perry Seagle died January 31, 1955, at his residence at Cameron Park Apartments. He was survived by his wife Sadie and two daughters, Miss Sara Gardner Seagle of Baltimore, Maryland, and Mrs. E.R.S. (Eleanor) Cole of Greenwich, Connecticut. Funeral services were held at Christ Church and burial was in Oakwood Cemetery.[6]

DR. CLARENCE POE

Dr. Clarence Poe, longtime editor of *The Progressive Farmer* and a moving force in the South's agricultural and educational progress for more than half a century, died in October 1964. He was 83.

Dr. Poe was one of the South's most respected journalists and authors who earned a reputation as a champion of Southern farm people.

He was editor of *The Progressive Farmer* for 67 years and was active as the company's board chairman and senior editor right up to his fatal illness.

He joined the staff of the magazine at the age of 16, fresh out of the cotton fields of his native Chatham County, and became editor at 18. Four years later, in 1899, he formed The Progressive Farmer Co. and bought the magazine for $7,500. It had a circulation of 5,000 at the time.

Fourteen Southern farm publications merged with the magazine during the first 20 years of Dr. Poe's ownership, and in the 1960s *The Progressive Farmer* has a circulation of 1,500,000. With headquarters of the company in Birmingham, Ala., it had regional editorial offices in the Insurance Building in Raleigh.

Wrote Several Books

Dr. Poe was the author of several books. One of his last, published in 1963, was *My First 80 Years*. He also wrote *A Southerner in Europe*, *True Tales of the South at War*, and *Where Half the World is Waking Up*.

At the time of his death, he was working on two more books.

Asked once by a reporter what he considered to be his most important contribution to Southern agriculture, Dr. Poe replied:

"The campaign for 'two-arm' farming I carried on through speeches and articles. All agricultural wealth is based on two forms of production, crops and livestock. At the time I began my campaign, the South was using just 'one arm' (common and tobacco) and getting nothing from the other 'arm,' livestock."

---

[6] Adapted in part from the *News and Observer*, Raleigh, North Carolina, February 1, 1955. Courtesy of Olivia Raney Local History Library, Raleigh, NC.

Dr. Poe's formal education was limited to a few years in a one-room school and evening sessions in the home of his uncle, but he became a man of broad, self-instilled learning.

State Treasurer Edwin Gill, reviewing Dr. Poe's last published book, wrote, "If I were to attempt to name the best educated men in North Carolina today, I would certainly include Dr. Poe."

Dr. Poe received honorary doctorate degrees from several colleges, including Wake Forest, the University of North Carolina, N.C. State and Clemson.

Over the years, he was presented numerous awards for service to Southern agriculture. He was one of the recipients of the first annual North Carolina Awards presented earlier this year by Gov. Sanford.

The American Freedom Association presented Dr. Poe its World Peace Award in 1962.

From 1913 to 1921, he was a member of the State Board of Agriculture. He served on many State and national advisory boards.

In 1940, farmers of the State launched a movement to induce Dr. Poe to become a candidate for Governor. His supporters thought they might persuade him, but in the end he stuck to his first love, *The Progressive Farmer.*

For hobbies, Dr. Poe liked landscaping and gardening. He once called himself "an apostle of the crepe myrtle." He planted hundreds of crepe myrtles around Longview Gardens, an 800-acre estate which he turned into a residential subdivision.

One of Dr. Poe's heroes was Charles Brantley Aycock, North Carolina's great educational Governor at the turn of the century. In 1912, Dr. Poe married one of Aycock's daughters, Alice.

Mrs. Poe died about a year before her husband.

They were survived by a son, Charles Aycock Poe, and a daughter, Mrs. Gordon Smith, Jr., both of Raleigh; a sister, Mrs. George Moore of Gulf; seven grandchildren and one great-grandchild.[7]

VONNIE M. HICKS

Vonnie M. Hicks, Sr., was an Orange County native, born June 22, 1895. He was educated at the University of North Carolina at Chapel Hill

---

[7] Adapted from obituary, *News and Observer*, Raleigh, North Carolina, October 9, 1964. Courtesy of North Carolina Collection, University of North Carolina, Chapel Hill, North Carolina.

and at Jefferson Medical College in Philadelphia. His medical specialty was ophthalmology.

He began practicing in Raleigh in 1921 and was a consulting physician at Wake Memorial Hospital and at Rex Hospital. He was a partner in the eye, ear, nose and throat firm of doctors Lewis, Wright, Hicks, and Gibson, located in the Citizens National Bank building.

Vonnie married Jessie Greggs in 1926. They lived at 1539 Iredell Drive in Raleigh.

Dr. Hicks was a member of the Raleigh Academy of Medicine and a life member of the American College of Surgeons. He was president of the Wake County Medical Society in 1943.

He was the supervising ophthalmologist of the North Carolina Commission for the Blind until his retirement in 1969.

Vonnie Hicks died November 28, 1971, with funeral services at St. Michael's Episcopal Church, conducted by Reverends James W. Beckwith and B. Daniel Sapp.

Surviving Vonnie were two sons, Dr. Vonnie M. Hicks, Jr., and Greig Lee Hicks; a daughter, Mrs. Elizabeth Jane Hicks McCrary; nine grandchildren and two great-grandchildren, all of Raleigh; a brother, Tom L. Hicks of Newberry, South Carolina; and a sister, Mrs. Harold Lewis of Winston-Salem.[8]

DR. WARREN W. WAY

Dr. Warren W. Way, rector of St. Mary's School in Raleigh from 1918 to 1929, died on June 11, 1941, in Tryon.

Dr. Way was born in Irvington, Ill., in 1869. He won his A.B. degree from Hobart College in 1897 and in 1899 he was ordained to the ministry, after having attended General Theological Seminary in New York.

Following service in several parishes, Dr. Way became rector at St. Luke's Episcopal Church in Salisbury in 1904. He served there until 1918, when he became rector at St. Mary's. It was while he was at St. Mary's that Dr. Way's fame spread throughout the State. He made a deep impression upon the students who came under his pastoral care, and they never forgot him.

In 1929, Dr. Way became rector of St. James Episcopal Church at

---

[8] Adapted in part from the *News and Observer*, Raleigh, North Carolina, November 30, 1971. Courtesy of the Olivia Raney Local History Library, Raleigh, North Carolina.

Atlantic City, N.J. He retired in 1942 and moved to Tryon, where he filled the pulpit at the Church of the Holy Cross. He also served at the pulpit of Episcopal churches at Columbia and Saluda, S.C.

Among the degrees held by Dr. Way were an M.A. degree awarded him in 1924 by the University of Chicago and a D.D. degree awarded by the University of the South in 1929.

He was survived by his wife, the former Louisa Atkinson Smith of Staunton. Va.; a daughter Evelyn Way, assistant professor of Latin at the University of Mississippi; two sons, Sgt. Warren W. Way, Jr., of the U.S. Army, stationed at Duke University, and Capt. Roger A. Way, Medical Corps, U.S. Army, stationed at Starke General Hospital, Charleston, S.C.[9]

JOHN A. ELLIS

Dr. John A. Ellis, 78, of Arbutus Drive, former pastor of Pullen Memorial Baptist Church, died at Rex Hospital in Raleigh in July 1960.

Dr. Ellis served as pastor of Pullen Memorial here from 1919 to 1929. For 22 years he was pastor of the First Baptist Church in Sherman, Texas. He was called from retirement in 1951 and served as pastor of Tabernacle Baptist Church here for nearly five years.

Dr. Ellis attended Campbell College and received his AB and MA degrees from Wake Forest College. He received his Theological Th.D. degrees from the Southern Baptist Theological Seminary in Louisville, Ky. Wake Forest conferred an honorary doctor of divinity degree on him.

Dr. Ellis also served as pastor of the First Baptist Church in Dunn and as a U.S. Army chaplain during World War I. He served as a member of the Executive Committee of the Baptist General Convention of Texas and was president of the North Texas Baptist Encampment. He was twice elected chairman of the board of the Biblical Recorder.

Surviving were his wife, the former Helen Becker of Roanoke, Va.; two daughters, Mrs. William Bond of Vernob, Texas, and Mrs. J. P. Livingston of Richardson, Texas; two sons, John A. Jr., of Princeton, N. J., and Leland of Grifton; two sisters, Mrs. Ruth Murchison of Rocky Mount and Mrs. Will Maclean of High Point; one brother, Caswell Ellis of Greenville, S.C.; and 11 grandchildren.

Funeral services were held at the Tabernacle Baptist Church by the Rev. James F. Heaton, the Rev. W. W. Finlator, pastor of Pullen

---

[9] Adapted from obituary, *News and Observer*, Raleigh, North Carolina, June 12, 1941. Courtesy of North Carolina Collection, University of North Carolina, Chapel Hill, North Carolina.

Memorial, and Dr. C. C. Carpenter of the Baptist State Convention. Dr. Ellis was buried in the Restlawn Memory Gardens.[10]

BROWN SHEPHERD

Raleigh attorney Sylvester Brown Shepherd of 2411 Country Club Drive died on April 25, 1946, at Raleigh's Rex Hospital.

Mr. Shepherd was born August 6, 1876, in Washington, N.C., son of the late James E. Shepherd, Chief Justice of the North Carolina Supreme Court, and Elizabeth Brown Shepherd, sister of the late Associate Justice George H. Brown of the State Supreme Court.

The family moved to Raleigh in 1889. Mr. Shepherd attended Morson and Denson's School here and the Horner Military Academy at Oxford. He was graduated from Carolina in 1897, where he was a member of D. K. E. and Gim Ghouls. He was licensed to practice law in February 1898. He was associated with his father in the firm of Shepherd and Shepherd, until the latter's death. Mr. Shepherd continued in active practice until a few years before his death when his varied business largely absorbed his attentions. Mr. Shepherd had extensive property holdings here.

In 1935 he addressed the American Bar Association in Los Angeles, Cal., on the subject of uniform suretyship laws. He was president of the Wake County Bar Association in 1937, and at the time of his death was president of the board of directors of the Olivia Raney Library. He was a director of the Atlantic Fire Insurance Company. A communicant of the Episcopal Church, Mr. Shepherd for many years was a vestryman of the Church of the Good Shepherd, and he formerly taught a class of boys in the Sunday school of the church.

The work of the Thompson Orphanage also engaged his attention. He held membership in the Raleigh Chamber of Commerce, the American Bar Association, the North Carolina Bar Association, the Wake County Bar Association, the International Association of Insurance Counsel, the Carolina Country Club and the Neusco Fishing Club.

Mr. Shepherd was Wake's representative in the lower House of the General Assembly in 1919.

In 1900, he married Lilla May Vass, daughter of the late Major

---

[10] Adapted from obituary, *News and Observer*, Raleigh, North Carolina, July 5, 1960. Courtesy of North Carolina Collection, University of North Carolina, Chapel Hill, North Carolina.

W. W. Vass.

Surviving were his wife; a daughter, Mrs. T. Roney Williamson of Lawton, Okla.; and two sons, James E. Shepherd of Washington and William Vass Shepherd of Coral Gables, Fla.

Funeral services were held at the Church of the Good Shepherd with the Rev. J. McDowell Dick, rector, officiating. He was buried in Oakwood Cemetery.[11]

DR. CLARENCE A. SHORE

Dr. Clarence A. Shore, director of the State Laboratory of Hygiene for 25 years, died on February 10, 1933.

Dr. Shore was prominently connected with the medical profession in this section of the country and was a recognized authority on the treatment of the disease of hydrophobia.

He came to Raleigh 25 years ago from the University of North Carolina, where he was an instructor in pathology, to take up his duties as director of the laboratory. Within several years, the laboratory had gained a reputation of national standing.

Dr. Shore was a graduate of the University of North Carolina, receiving his B.S. degree there, and from Johns Hopkins University, where he received his M.D. degree. In 1929, the degree of Doctor of Laws was conferred upon him by the University of North Carolina.

Dr. Shore was selected as one of two delegates to attend a conference on the treatment of rabies at the Pasteur Institute, Paris, in 1927. The selection was made by the United States Public Health Service.

In 1932, Dr. Shore was elected president of the Tri-State Medical Association, an organization whose membership comprises physicians in North and South Carolina and Virginia. He was scheduled to have presided over the Association's annual convention in Greenville, SC., the week before he died.

Born on November 26, 1873, in Winston-Salem, Dr. Shore was the son of Washington and Lavinia Elizabeth Shore. He received his early education training in a private school at Winston-Salem and at the Salem Boys' School before entering the University of North Carolina.

He was a member of a number of national and state medical

---

[11] Adapted from obituary, *News and Observer*, Raleigh, North Carolina, April 26, 1946. Courtesy of North Carolina Collection, University of North Carolina, Chapel Hill, North Carolina.

organizations, in addition to social and honorary fraternities. He was well known as a writer on technical subjects in connection with the medical profession and also as a speaker at medical association meetings.

Dr. Shore was survived by his widow, formerly Miss Ellen Dortch of Raleigh, and the following brothers and sisters: Mrs. Frank Meinung, Winston-Salem; Charles E. Shore, Miami, Florida; George D. Shore, Sumter, S.C.; Henry A. Shore, Washington, D.C.; Mrs. J. A. Seaber, Columbia, S.C.; Mrs. T. H. Siddell, Sumter, S.C.; and Dr. Howard J. Shore, Fort Dodge, Iowa.[12]

JOHN J. BLAIR

John J. Blair, prominent educator and civic leader of High Point and former resident of Raleigh, died in November 1937 in Charlotte. He was 77.

For many years Mr. Blair devoted much of his time and efforts to promoting the art movement in this State and was instrumental in bringing the Pfeiffer collection of paintings to North Carolina.

A close friend of the late Robert F. Pfeiffer, wealthy Philadelphian and native of Cabarrus County, N.C., Mr. Blair influenced him to will his collection to the State Art Society, and also to provide for considerable funds to come to North Carolina from the Pfeiffer estate upon the death of two heirs. Mr. Blair was the society's first president. Several of the paintings included in the collection were hung in the Executive Mansion and State buildings here. When a resident of Raleigh, Mr. Blair looked after their care personally. Until his health failed he was active in a movement to establish a State Art Gallery so that more private wealth would be attracted here in building up collections.

Mr. Blair, along with his brothers and sisters, gave High Point its impetus for its public park system, now regarded as one of the finest in the South. The land for Blair Park was the gift of this family to this city.

Mr. Blair was a member of a pioneer Quaker family in this section. He was born at the Blair homeplace here, a son of Soloman and Abigail Hunt Blair. He had been active in educational circles over the State, having served at one time as Superintendent of the Winston-Salem schools and later as Superintendent at Wilmington. After resigning at Wilmington Mr.

---

[12] Adapted from obituary, *News and Observer*, Raleigh, North Carolina, February 11, 1933. Courtesy of North Carolina Collection, University of North Carolina, Chapel Hill, North Carolina.

Blair directed construction of school buildings for the State, retiring five years ago because of his health.

Surviving were two brothers, David H. Blair of Washington, D.C. and High Point, and Colonel W. A. Blair of Winston-Salem, and four sisters, Misses Martha, Ada, Emma, and Elva Blair, all of High Point.[13]

THEODORE S. JOHNSON

Theodore S. Johnson, 65, wartime OPA director and rationing administrator for North Carolina, died on November 5, 1950, at the Veterans Hospital in Fayetteville.

Johnson, a former professor in the State College Civil Engineering Department, was active in local civic and church affairs over a long period of time.

Funeral services were conducted at the First Baptist Church in Raleigh with Dr. Broadus E. Jones and Dr. E. McNeill Poteat officiating, but Johnson was buried in Granville, Ohio.

West Virginian

He was born in Parkersburg, West Virginia, on July 28, 1885, the son of David Dye Johnson and Julia Dale Johnson. He was educated at Denison University, Ohio State, and Cornell.

Johnson joined the State College faculty in 1933. He resigned to become State director of the Office of Civilian Defense in June 1941. He was made State Rationing Administrator in January 1942, and became North Carolina's OPA director in May 1942.

He returned to the State College campus in March 1947, to become veterans adviser in charge of housing and liaison officer between the college administration and construction officials in the institution's permanent improvements program. He resigned that post when his health failed following the death of his wife in 1949.

He was a member and former president of the Raleigh Rotary Club, district governor of Rotary International, and chairman of the Rotary International committee on extension. He also served as a member of the Raleigh Housing Authority, a trustee of the Olivia Raney Library, as president of the Raleigh YMCA, and for two years as president of the Raleigh Civic Music Association.

---

[13] Adapted from obituary, *News and Observer*, Raleigh, North Carolina, November 14-15, 1937. Courtesy of North Carolina Collection, University of North Carolina, Chapel Hill, North Carolina.

A Baptist

He was a member of the board of deacons of the First Baptist Church, a member of the Raleigh Baptist City Council, and secretary of the North Carolina Baptist Foundation, Inc.

He was survived by a daughter, Mrs. Robert Llewellyn of Raleigh; a sister, Frances Dwight Johnson of Parkersburg, W.V.; and a brother, Dr. David Dale Johnson of Morgantown, W.V. His wife, the former Marion Grayson Rose, died in 1949.

Pallbearers at his funeral were Claude F. Gaddy, Willis G. Briggs, I. M. Bailey, Will Wyatt, Bunyan Tyner, and Carl W. Bengel. Honorary pallbearers were members of the Raleigh Rotary Club, the Raleigh Sandwich Club, and deacons of the First Baptist Church.[14]

CURRIN KEEBLE

Currin Greaves Keeble, the son of Horace Greaves Keeble and Annie Nelson Keeble, was born September 15, 1877, in Murfreesboro, Tennessee. He attended Wake Forest College and studied law at the University of North Carolina at Chapel Hill. He was a member of Sigma Nu fraternity.

He came to Raleigh around 1900 and taught at the Raleigh Male Academy, conducted at that time by Hugh A. Morson. A football game with North Carolina State in 1892 was the first for the latter.

According to the 1912 North Carolina State *Agromeck*, Keeble was an instructor in the English Department at that time.

In 1925 he married Mary Grimes Cowper and they lived at 501 North Blount Street in the dwelling known as Cowper House.

For some years Keeble practiced law. He served at one time on the Raleigh Board of Adjustment, a quasi-judicial board that hears requests for variances to zoning rules.

He was a deacon of the First Presbyterian Church. His obituary noted that he was a member of the Sandwich Club. For many years he served as trustee and treasurer of the Olivia Raney Library.

He was survived by his wife; three sisters, Misses Mary and Laura Keeble and Mrs. James Clayton of Murfreesboro, Tennessee; and a niece and a nephew.

---

[14] Adapted from obituary, *News and Observer*, Raleigh, North Carolina, November 6, 1950. Courtesy of North Carolina Collection, University of North Carolina, Chapel Hill, North Carolina.

Currin Keeble died at his home on July 13, 1954. His funeral was held there and he was buried in Oakwood Cemetery.[15]

ROBERT RUARK

Robert Ruark, a member of the bar at Raleigh, practicing as senior partner in the firm of Ruark & Ruark, was born in Southport, N.C., December 3, 1878, a son of James Buchanan and Sally Porter (Longest) Ruark. Ruark's father was a merchant of Southport who also served as president of the school board and helped to organize a private subscription school in Southport.

Robert Ruark was educated in private schools and under the direction of tutors. He spent two years in surveying in connection with the engineering department of the war forces, being on duty on Cape Fear River and on the construction of Fort Caswell, N.C. He enrolled as a law student in the University of North Carolina and won admission to the bar January 24, 1900. He began practicing in Wilmington, North Carolina, but spent the year 1903 in New York City as assistant to the general attorney of the Western Union Telegraph Company. Returning to North Carolina, he practiced law in Lexington in 1904-05 as a partner in the firm of McCrary & Ruark. Returning then to Wilmington, he was a member of Naeres & Ruark from 1906 until 1911 and thereafter practiced alone until 1920, when he became city attorney of Wilmington, filling the position for three terms, from 1920 to 1925. He next became associated in practice with W. B. Campbell, under the firm name Ruark & Campbell, specializing in insurance, admiralty and corporation law. In 1925 he came to Raleigh, where for four years he was a partner of A. J. Fletcher in the firm of Ruark & Fletcher. In 1929 that firm was dissolved and Mr. Ruark was joined by his son, Samuel W., under the firm name of Ruark & Ruark. They continued in general practice in the state and federal courts but made a specialty of insurance law.

On October 22, 1902, Mr. Ruark was united in marriage to Hettie Gibbons Westbrook of Faison, N.C. Robert Ruark's wife graduated from Greensboro College for Women and taught for one year prior to her marriage. Robert and Hettie had four children: Samuel Westbrook Ruark, an attorney in practice with his father; Robert James Ruark, a physician in Raleigh; Henry Gibbons Ruark, a Methodist pastor; and their only

---

[15] Adapted in part from the *News and Observer*, Raleigh, North Carolina, July 14, 1954. Courtesy of the Olivia Raney Local History Library, Raleigh, NC.

daughter, Sarah Frances Ruark Moore.

Mr. Ruark was particularly active in the work of the Methodist church and Sunday school throughout his adult life, first in Grace Methodist Episcopal Church at Wilmington, then at the Edenton Street Methodist Episcopal Church and the Hayes-Barton Methodist Church in Raleigh. He manifested a keen interest in civic and public affairs. For years, he was active in the councils of the Democratic party and was chairman of the advisory committee in Governor Hoey's campaign. He was a member of the State Democratic Executive Committee. He served as a past president of the Wake County Bar Association, spent three years on the grievance committee of the N.C. State Bar Association, and belonged to the American Bar Association as well as the International Association of Insurance Counsel, of which he was a past member of the executive committee and served as president in 1939.

Robert Ruark died in 1958, having retired from his law practice several years earlier. His law firm still survives and flourishes under the name Young, Moore & Henderson, named in part for Joseph Calhoun Moore, Jr., husband of Sarah Frances Ruark Moore, Robert Ruark's only daughter.[16]

HARRISON PANTON

Harrison Douglas Panton was born May 21, 1891, in Guelph, Canada, but was raised in Boydton, Virginia. His parents were J. Hayes Panton and Fanny B. Harrison.

He was a graduate of Virginia Polytechnic Institute in Blacksburg and of the Cornell Graduate School in 1914.

Harrison Panton married Alston Veree Dargan in November 1919. They had two children, Mary Jerman Panton (later Mrs. Guy Crampton, Jr.) and James Harrison Panton.

For many years he was an engineer for the West Penn Power Company at Pittsburgh. In the early 1920s, he was an electrical engineer for the Yadkin River Power Company in Rockingham, North Carolina. According to a *Raleigh City Directory*, Panton was then working for the operating department of Carolina Power and Light Company in 1922 and living at 605 N. Bloodworth Street. According to the April 5, 1923 *Cornell Alumni News,* Panton, a "registered engineer, opened an office in Raleigh,

---

[16] Henderson, Archibald, *North Carolina: The Old North State and the New,* Lewis Publishing Company, 1941. Provided by the Ruark family.

N.C., for the general practice of electrical and mechanical engineering."

Panton was a retired Major in the Army Reserve.

Harrison Panton died January 4, 1965, at age 72. He was buried in the National Cemetery in Raleigh. Survivors included his son, James Panton of Raleigh; his daughter, Mrs. Guy Crampton, Jr., of Raleigh; and five grandchildren.[17]

GEORGE CONNOR

George Whitfield Connor was born October 24, 1872, in Wilson, N.C. His father was Henry G. Connor, attorney, bank president, politician, and jurist. George had twelve siblings. Two of his brothers gained prominence in their own right: H. G. Connor, Jr., who was a lawyer and legislator, and Robert D. W. Connor, who became the first Archivist of the United States.

George attended the University of North Carolina, where he was a member of the Philanthropic Society, one of the campus oratory groups. Graduated in 1891, he was one of a few students to receive "prizes" during commencement, when he was awarded the "Rep. Medal," presented by the Hon. Rufus A. Doughton of Alleghany.

George was a member of Sigma Alpha Epsilon and the Knights of Pythias. He was offered membership on the Trustees of the University of North Carolina, but declined the position. He and his wife Bessie lived in Raleigh at 825 Holt Drive in the Hayes-Barton neighborhood.

George Connor was elected as a member of the North Carolina State House of Representatives from Wilson County in 1909 and served until 1913. He also served briefly as the Speaker of the North Carolina State House of Representatives in 1913, resigning after the session of January 8 to March 12.

Elected as an associate justice to the North Carolina State Supreme Court in 1927, he served eleven years. Connor died while in office on April 23, 1938. Upon his death, Governor Clyde Roark Hoey delivered a profound eulogy. He wrote that George Connor "represented the best in life and thought of North Carolina. His whole life has been given to service of the Commonwealth, as a lawyer, legislator, Superior Court judge, and Supreme Court justice, and in each instance he served

---

[17] Adapted in part from obituary, *News and Observer*, Raleigh, North Carolina, January 5, 1965, courtesy of the Olivia Raney Local History Library, Raleigh, North Carolina; *1922 Raleigh City Directory*.

with outstanding ability and with fine consecration."[18]

JUDGE MICHAEL SCHENCK

Judge Michael Schenck, 71-year old jurist who served for 24 years as Superior Court judge and State Supreme Court justice, died on November 5, 1948, ten months after he stepped into retirement.

"His opinions," a former colleague said, "will stand as his monument."

Governor Cherry, in a formal statement said, "North Carolina has lost one of her ablest citizens in the death of Former Justice Michael Schenck. As district solicitor, and as Superior and Supreme Court justice, he has rendered his State valuable service over a long span of years, and I join with his many friends in mourning his passing."

Resigned In January

In ill health for more a year, Judge Schenck resigned from the Supreme Court January 1948.

Funeral services were held at Raleigh's Christ Church. Bishop Edwin A. Penick officiated, assisted by the Rev. Ray Holder, the rector. Judge Schenck was buried in Hendersonville.

Honorary pallbearers included members of the Supreme Court bench and of the Council of State.

Active pallbearers were Adrian Newton, Dillard Gardner, Hughes Rhodes, Harry Sample, John Strong, Clyde A. Erwin, Pat Kimzey and Joseph B. Cheshire, Sr.

Chief Justice Walter P. Stacy with whom Judge Schenck served for many years, wrote in a statement that the State had suffered a "great loss."

"In the death of Judge Schenck," the statement said, "a great loss has come to the people of the State whom he served so long and well.

"None can appreciate his worth more accurately than the members of the Supreme Court with whom he was associated and who knew intimately his qualities as citizen and public official.

"He was diligent and painstaking, urbane and always courteous. His opinions will stand as his monument. Truly, a great public servant has fallen."

---

[18] Hoey, Clyde Roark, *Addresses, Letters and Papers of Clyde Roark Hoey, Governor of North Carolina,* edited by David Leroy Corbitt, Kensington Publ., 2005, p. 430; University of North Carolina, *North Carolina University Magazine,* Vol. 6-7, pp. 253. 287, 289; www.politicalgraveyard.com/bio/connor.html accessed 11 July 2010;

Judge Schenck was born in Lincolnton on December 11, 1876. He received his early education in Greensboro public schools and Oak Ridge Institute. He received his academic and professional education at the University of North Carolina and was admitted to the bar in 1903.

Served in Army

As a young lawyer, he practiced first in Hendersonville. Within four years he had been elected mayor of Hendersonville, a post he held from 1907 to 1909. Later, from 1913 to 1918, he was solicitor of the 18th Judicial District, leaving that to enter the Army in 1918 as a major in the Judge Advocate General's Department.

In 1924 Governor Cameron Morrison appointed him to the Superior Court as judge for the 18th Judicial District. From 1931 to 1932, he was a member of the Commission which drafted the North Carolinas State Constitution.

His appointment to the Supreme Court came in May 1934, under administration of Governor Ehringhaus, to fill a vacancy created by death of Associate Justice W. J. Adams.

Judge Schenck took part in the work of several organizations, chiefly the Masonic Lodge and American Legion.

In 1938, in recognition of his service in the court, the University of North Carolina awarded him the honorary degree of doctor of laws.

Judge Schenck was survived by his wife, the former Miss Rose Few, whom he married in 1909; a son, Michael Schenck, Jr., of Raleigh; and two daughters, Mrs. Rosemary S. Vaughan of Raleigh and Mrs. T.M. Ripley, Jr., of Aberdeen; and seven grandchildren.[19]

WILLIS BRIGGS

Willis Grandy Briggs of Raleigh, one of the State's best-known attorneys and an authoritative Raleigh historian, died in February 1954 at Rex Hospital. He was 78.

Mr. Briggs, long the Republican member of the Wake County Board of Elections, was a native and lifelong resident of Raleigh. Member of a pioneer Raleigh family, he was the son of the late Thomas Henry and Sarah G. Briggs of Raleigh.

Born in Raleigh on October 9, 1875, Mr. Briggs attended local schools and received his AB degree from Wake Forest College in 1896. He

---

[19] Adapted from obituary, *News and Observer*, Raleigh, North Carolina, November 6, 1948. Courtesy of North Carolina Collection, University of North Carolina, Chapel Hill, North Carolina.

also attended Wake Forest law school and was admitted to the bar in 1915.

In addition to his wide range of activities in the law and political fields, Mr. Briggs was an active worker in church, social and civic programs. He was a financial trustee and member of the Board of Deacons of the First Baptist Church, of which his great-grandfather, John J. Briggs, was a founder in 1812.

Mr. Briggs served as postmaster here from 1906 to 1914. Immediately after that, he was chosen as City Court prosecutor, a position he filled from 1915 until 1921.

From 1917 through 1918, Mr. Briggs served as member and secretary of the Raleigh Exemption Board of World War I.

When he left the prosecutor's post in 1921, Mr. Briggs became assistant U.S. attorney for the Eastern District. He held this post until 1930.

Other Honors

In 1934 he was Republican nominee for associate justice of the State Supreme Court and in 1938 was the GOP nominee for Congress from the Fourth District. In 1936 he was president of the Wake County Bar Association and in 1938 Mr. Briggs was elected president of the Seventh District of the State Bar Association.

He was a former member of the executive committee of the N.C. State Literary and Historical Association and was a past-president of the N.C. Society of Sons of the American Revolution.

Mr. Briggs was a member of the Carolina Country Club, Sandwich Club, Torch Club, Executives Club, Raleigh Bird Club and Raleigh History Club. He also was a member of the Raleigh Little Theater, an organization in which he always professed a keen interest.

As a historian of Raleigh and this area, Mr. Briggs perhaps was without a peer, and he gave generously of his time in helping researchers and others in gathering factual data on events and families connected with the Capital City. He was noted, too, for his humor and the numerous anecdotes about old-timers he had stored in his memory. He contributed frequently to newspapers, particularly articles on history.

Following in the footsteps of his father and grandfather, Mr. Briggs served as president of the Oakwood Cemetery Association.

Up to the time of his death, he was active in the law firm of Briggs and West here.

He was survived by two daughters, Dr. Sarah Briggs of Chambersburg, Pa., and Mrs. R. Dulany Furlong of Raleigh; a granddaughter; and a foster sister, Miss Bessie Brown of Raleigh.

Funeral services were held at the First Baptist Church, with the pastor, the Rev. Broadus E. Jones, officiating. He was buried at Oakwood.

Members of the Raleigh Bar Association served as honorary

pallbearers.[20]

I. M. BAILEY

I. M. Bailey, Raleigh lawyer, former legislator and one-time member of the Corporation Commission, forerunner of today's State Utilities Commission, died on July 4, 1951.

He was 59 years old.

He had practiced law in Raleigh since he left the old Corporation Commission in 1930 and had built up an extensive practice. He served as North Carolina counsel for the Atlantic Greyhound Corporation and as general counsel for the State Bankers Association and the North Carolina Merchants Association for a number of years.

Johnston Native

Isaac Mayo Bailey was born in Johnston County on October 28, 1891, the son of the late James Ruffin and Mary Jane Smith Bailey.

After receiving his A.B. degree from the University of North Carolina in 1914, he served as principal of the high school in Jacksonville, N.C., for three years. During that time, he also studied law and was admitted to the bar in 1918.

He represented Onslow County in the General Assembly of 1925 after practicing law in Jacksonville for eight years. After his legislative term, he became general counsel and assistant commissioner of the Corporation Commission, serving from April 1925 to March 1929. Then he was appointed a member of the commission by Governor O. Max Gardner and served in this capacity until February 1930, when he again became general counsel for the commission. He held this post until July 1931.

Leader In Bar

Mr. Bailey took the lead in successful efforts by North Carolina lawyers to establish the North Carolina State Bar and separate the licensing of attorneys from the Supreme Court. In recognition of his efforts, the State Bar elected him its first president and he served two terms, 1933 to 1935.

He has been president of the First Federal Savings and Loan Association here for a number of years and had served as president of the Raleigh Chamber of Commerce. He also was president of the Raleigh Community Chest In 1933.

Shortly after World War II, he was elected governor of Rotary

---

[20] Adapted from obituary, *News and Observer*, Raleigh, North Carolina, February 25, 1954. Courtesy of North Carolina Collection, University of North Carolina, Chapel Hill, North Carolina.

District 189. Previously, he had served at vice president of the Raleigh Rotary Club in 1930-31 and president of the club in 1933-34.

During and after World War II, Mr. Bailey was State Chairman of the government's bond sales campaign.

He was an active member and former vestryman of the Church of the Good Shepherd.

He was a Mason, a Shriner and a Woodman.

At the time of his death, Mr. Bailey was practicing law in partnership with a son, James Ruffin Bailey. During his legal career in Raleigh, he had been associated at varying times with a number of attorneys, including William C. Lassiter, William Wyatt, Jr., Clem B. Holding and Allen Langston.

Mrs. Bailey was the former Ida Thompson of Creswell. They were married December 31, 1914.

Surviving in addition to Mrs. Bailey were four children, Mrs. Ida Hassell Bailey Lavin of Fort Leavenworth, Kansas, I. M. Bailey, Jr., of Slimane, French Morocco, North Africa, Dr. Jean Bailey Brooks of Greensboro, and J. Ruffin Bailey of Raleigh; two grandchildren; a brother, Leon W. Bailey of Charlotte; and a sister, Mrs. Palmer Black of Charlotte.

Funeral services were conducted at the Church of the Good Shepherd, officiated by the Rev. J. McDowell Dick, rector of the church.[21]

FRANCIS PASCHAL

Joel Francis Paschal was born at Wake Forest in 1916. He was the son of G. W. Paschal, a Baptist professor, who taught Latin and Greek at Wake Forest College. Francis was the seventh child in a family of six boys and four girls. He entered school at age six but was quickly promoted to the fourth grade. He entered college in 1931 and was a member of the golf team. He received the B.A. degree in 1935 and at age 19 entered the Wake Forest Law School, being awarded the LLB degree in 1938.

After practicing law and studying at the University of Chicago, he became a law professor at Wake Forest at age 23, the youngest in the U.S. Around 1942 he received a masters degree from Princeton.

In 1942 he was commissioned an ensign in the U.S. Navy and served in the Pacific area. After the war he returned to Princeton where he

---

[21] Adapted from obituary, *News and Observer*, Raleigh, North Carolina, July 5, 1951. Courtesy of North Carolina Collection, University of North Carolina, Chapel Hill, North Carolina.

taught and in 1948 got his Ph.D. in politics, with his thesis published as a book with title *Mister Justice Sutherland: A Man against the State.*

When he came back to North Carolina he took a position at Duke with a newly created North Carolina Commission for the Improvement of Administration of Justice. This organization provided the State with a unified judicial system.

In 1951, Francis was practicing law in Raleigh in the office of Joseph B. Cheshire, Jr. He was executive secretary of the Judicial Council, was treasurer of the North Carolina World Federalists, and was writing a book on the analysis of different approaches to the Constitution.

Paschal's wife Primrose was a talented designer, artist, teacher, and writer. She was featured in the same newspaper article as her husband.

Francis Paschal died on January 10, 1991, and was buried in Oakwood Cemetery.[22]

CORNELIUS G. BRENNECKE

Dr. Cornelius G. Brennecke, 48, head of the Electrical Engineering Department at North Carolina State College since 1945, died in Raleigh in August 1954.

A nationally known teacher, physicist, and engineer, Dr. Brennecke came to State College from Lehigh University in Bethlehem, Pa., where he directed the university's work in electronics and communications.

For six years prior to his position on the Lehigh faculty, he was a member of the Toledo University faculty where he directed the training of engineering aides for the U.S. Army Signal Corps.

A native of New York City, he was educated at Columbia University, earning his A.B., B.S., and E.E. degrees, and at New York University, earning his Ph.D. degree.

Dr. Carey H. Bostian, State College chancellor, said "The loss of Dr. C. G. Brennecke to our State College family and to our North Carolina people will be keenly felt, especially by those who knew and admired him personally. He was a fine, cultured gentleman, a great teacher and scientist, an able, understanding administrator."

He worked for three years as a design engineer for the Radio

---

[22] Adapted from "Tar Heels of the Week: The Francis Paschals," *News and Observer*, Raleigh, North Carolina, October 7, 1951. Courtesy of North Carolina Collection, University of North Carolina, Chapel Hill, North Carolina

Corporation of America. He also spent five years doing graduate research work at NYU, largely in atomic physics and in the conducting of electricity through dielectrics. He received wide recognition for his work on artificial nuclear disintegration by high voltage proton beams.

Later he did research work on electronic devices for decreasing hazards of mining operations. With two associates, he was granted a U.S. patent on a safety device for mining.

He was appointed State College representative on the Council of the Oak Ridge Institute of Nuclear Studies in 1949.

He delivered a principal research report at an annual meeting of the American Institute of Mining and Metallurgical Engineers in Chicago. He was elected, president of the State College Chapter of Sigma Xi, America's highest honor society in the general sciences.

He was also a member of many other technical and professional societies, including the American Association for Engineering Education, the N.C. Society of Engineering Education, the N.C. Society of Engineering, the Raleigh Engineers Club, and the American Institute of Electrical Engineers. He was a fellow of the Institute of Radio Engineers and a fellow of the American Institute of Electrical Engineers. In addition, he was a member of Phi Beta Phi at State College.

Dr. J. Harold Lampe, School of Engineering dean, expressed deep regret over the untimely death of the school's Electrical Engineering head.

He helped to organize the North Carolina-Virginia Section of the Institute of Radio Engineers, serving as its president in 1948 and its vice president for the two preceding years. Numerous scientific articles by Dr. Brennecke appeared in technical publications.

He once served as chairman of the Toledo, Ohio, Section and manager of the Bethlehem, Penn., District of the American Institute of Electrical Engineers. He also did consulting work in acoustics, sound reproduction, and illumination.

In addition to his professional affiliations, Dr. Brennecke was a member of the Lutheran Church and the American Guild of Organists. He was an accomplished organist and served as church organist in a Bethlehem Lutheran Church. He was also president of the Church Council of the Lutheran Church.

He was survived by his wife, the former Ruby J. Kaulbach of Conquerall Mills, Nova Scotia; one daughter, Elizabeth, 12; and one son, Cornelius Godfrey Jr., 6.

Funeral services were held at Holy Trinity Lutheran Church in Raleigh. Dr. Brennecke was buried in Montlawn Cemetery.

Active pallbearers were C. D. Arthur, Arthur Brown, H. F. Wilson,

William F. Troxler, W. D. Stevenson Jr., and G. D. Arndt.

Honorary pallbearers were all members of the State College Electrical Engineering Department.[23]

ADDISON HICKMAN

Charles Addison Hickman was born June 11, 1916, in Sioux City, Iowa. He graduated from East High School there in 1934 and obtained at the University of Iowa the degrees B.A., M.A., and Ph.D. He also studied at Columbia University.

He was an instructor in economics at Stetson University in Deland, Florida, 1938-1940. In the period 1940-1950 he worked up from instructor to professor at State University of Iowa. This was interrupted during World War II, when in 1944-1945 he was attached to the U.S. Army as an expediter.

Dr. Hickman was a prolific researcher and writer, with many articles and books on economics topics to his credit.

He was appointed Head of the Department of Economics at North Carolina State in 1953 and became Dean of the School of General Studies in 1956. In 1960 he left NCSU, accepting an endowed professorship (the Vandeveer Chair of Economics) at Southern Illinois University. Later, 1963-1964, he served as Dean of the Graduate School.

He was married to the former Dorothy P. Hoeffler, with whom he had three children—Mary, Mark, and Paul.[24]

EDWIN GILL

Edwin Maurice Gill, lawyer and public official, was born in 1899 in Laurinburg, N.C., the son of Thomas Jeffries and Mamie North Gill. After attending local schools, he entered Trinity College in 1922 but left in 1924 after passing the bar examination. He established his practice in Laurinburg, and was elected to represent Scotland County in the General

---

[23] Adapted from obituary, *News and Observer*, Raleigh, North Carolina, August 3, 1954. Courtesy of North Carolina Collection, University of North Carolina, Chapel Hill, North Carolina.

[24] Adapted from obituary, *News and Observer*, Raleigh, North Carolina, April 25, 1953; February 28, 1956; and March 5, 1960. Courtesy of North Carolina Collection, University of North Carolina, Chapel Hill, North Carolina.

Assembly in 1929 and 1931. In the legislature he was a member of the subcommittees that drafted the state's local government act and the bill authorizing the state to take over the construction and maintenance of county roads. He also supported legislation for the Australian ballot, workmen's compensation, university consolidation, and benefits for the blind.

On July 1, 1931, after the General Assembly adjourned, Gill became private secretary to Governor O. Max Gardner and remained in that post during Gardner's administration. Afterward he compiled the governor's letters and papers for publication. In 1933 Governor J. C. B. Ehringhaus appointed Gill to head the newly created North Carolina Paroles Commission, a position he filled until 1942. Organizing the office and adopting procedures for the commission, he created a model agency that was widely copied throughout the nation and commented upon favorably by federal officials. Between 1942 and 1949 Gill served as Commissioner of Revenue by appointment of Governor J. Melville Broughton; at the end of that period he joined a law firm in Washington, D.C., founded by former Governor Gardner. President Harry S Truman named him Collector of Internal Revenue in North Carolina in 1950. He left the post in 1953 when he was appointed State Treasurer by Governor William B. Umstead. Thereafter Gill was elected to this office until he retired in 1976. Under his direction, the state attained the highest possible credit rating. It was he who coined the phrase, "In North Carolina, we have made a habit of good government." Gill himself was often referred to as "Mr. Integrity."

In addition to his public offices, Gill was also a member of and an officer in various organizations including the State Banking Commission, Local Government Commission, Tax Review Board, Sinking Fund Commission, Capital Planning Commission, Southeastern State Probation and Parole Association, American Prison Association, and National Tax Association.

Mr. Gill, as everyone called him, was a brilliant man, well-read and a lover of the arts. As a young man Gill studied for a year at the New York School of Fine and Applied Arts. He painted as a hobby and was a zealous supporter of the North Carolina Museum of Art, serving as an active and effectual member of the board of trustees and a director of the State Art Society. He was also interested in music and was considered a respectable pianist and organist. An indefatigable reader, he was an avid but generous book collector. Many libraries in the state benefited from his gifts.

Gill was a Methodist and taught Sunday school at the Edenton Street Methodist Church in Raleigh. He was also a Democrat. Both Duke

University and Campbell College awarded him honorary degrees. He never married.

Edwin Gill died in July 1978.[25]

GEORGE GEOGHEGAN

George Pinckney Geoghegan, 74, a retired regional vice president of Wachovia Bank and Trust Co. and a member of the Raleigh-Durham Airport Authority, died in February 1969.

Geoghegan, long a leading figure in the city's financial and civic circles, won warm community admiration in late years for continuing his active role in current affairs despite severe arthritis.

A native of Danville, Va., he came to Raleigh in 1936 to become vice president of the Wachovia branch and later was promoted to senior vice president. In 1955 he became regional vice president in charge of bank operations in the Raleigh-Goldsboro-Wilmington area. He retired in 1960.

He continued on the board of Occidental Life Insurance Co., a post he had held from 1937 until February 1965 and was secretary of the local airport authority until 1967. He was made an authority member in 1949.

Chamber President

He was a member of the N.C. State University Development Council from 1945 to 1965, was president of the Raleigh Chamber of Commerce in 1947, president of the Capital Area Development Association in 1957, president of the North Carolina Association of Real Estate Boards in 1933 and executive vice president of the Citizens for Preservation of Constitutional Government in 1962.

He was a member of the Carolina Country Club, White Memorial Presbyterian Church, the Rotary Club, the State Art Society, the State Music Society and the American Legion.

In March 1962 he received the honorary degree of doctor of humanities from N.C. State University.

Geoghegan was listed in *Who's Who in American Commerce and Industry* from 1945 to 1965, was Tar Heel of the Week in the *News and Observer* in March 1950 and received the "Senior Citizens Award" of the Raleigh Chamber of Commerce in 1965.

Funeral services were conducted at White Memorial Presbyterian Church by the Rev. Polk Moffett and Dr. H. Edwin Pickard. He was buried

---

[25] Powell, William S., "Edwin Maurice Gill," *Dictionary of North Carolina Biography, Vol. 3, H-K*, edited by William S. Powell, Chapel Hill: University of North Carolina Press, 1988.

in Oakwood Cemetery.

He was survived by his wife, Mrs. Helen Ruth Dodge Geoghegan; two brothers, William A. Geoghegan of Martinsville, Va., and John T. Geoghegan of Wayne, Pa.; sisters, Mrs. Thomas Morris of Martinsville, Va., Mrs. Scott Conkling of New York, N.Y., Mrs. Henry Myers of Greensboro and Miss Aileen Geoghegan of Charlottesville, Va.; a daughter, Mrs. Sydnor M. White of Raleigh; and a son, George Dodge Geoghegan of Raleigh.[26]

CARLYLE CAMPBELL

Teacher and college president, Dr. Arthur Carlyle Campbell was born in Buies Creek in 1894 to James Archibald and Cornelia Frances Pearson Campbell. His preparatory education was at Buies Creek Academy and he received A.B. and M.A. degrees from Wake Forest College in 1911 and 1916, respectively. He also studied at Columbia University during the period 1920-23. The University of South Carolina awarded him the honorary LL.D. degree in 1929 and Wake Forest did the same in 1950. During the years 1911-17 and 1919-20 he was an instructor in English at Buies Creek Academy. In 1923 he joined the faculty of Coker College, Hartsville, S.C., as professor of English and head of the department and during the years 1925-36 he was president of Coker College. From 1937 until 1939 he was professor and head of the English department at North Carolina State College, and in 1939 he became president of Meredith College, a post he filled until his retirement in 1966. Campbell served a term as president of the North Carolina College Conference and of the Southern Association of Colleges and Secondary Schools. He was also a member of the State Education Commission, 1947-49, and an advisory member of the North Carolina Board of Higher Education, 1962-65.

In 1917-18 Campbell was the ranking band sergeant of the Field Artillery Band and in 1918 was commissioned second lieutenant in the field artillery. During the year 1946-47 he was president of the North Carolina Literary and Historical Association. He was a member of Phi Beta Kappa, a Democrat, and a Baptist. In 1925 he was married to Marion Lee Newman and they were the parents of Virginia Lee (Mrs. Randy Stanford) and Carlyle. He died in 1977 and was buried in Buies Creek.[27]

---

[26] Adapted from obituary, *News and Observer*, Raleigh, North Carolina, February 17, 1969. Courtesy of North Carolina Collection, University of North Carolina, Chapel Hill, North Carolina.

[27] Powell, William S., "Arthur Carlyle Campbell," *Dictionary of North Carolina Biography, Vol. 1, A-C*, edited by William S. Powell, Chapel Hill: University of

CHARLES POE

Charles Aycock Poe was born in Raleigh on April 18, 1913. He was the son of distinguished parents, Clarence Poe, editor of the *Progressive Farmer*, and the former Alice Aycock, daughter of Governor Charles Brantley Aycock.

Charlie attended the University of North Carolina at Chapel Hill, where he was a stellar intramural athlete, excelling in football, basketball, softball, and tennis. He made Phi Beta Kappa as a junior, was editor of the literary *Carolina Magazine* as well as a member of the Board of Editors of the *North Carolina Law Review*, was president of the Law School Association, and was a member of Golden Fleece. He received the A.B. degree in 1935 and the law degree in 1938.

Poe practiced law for three years in association with Governor J. C. B. Ehringhaus, then served in the FBI from May 1941 to October 1945. He formed the law firm Harris and Poe with his old friend William C. ("Buck") Harris. The firm was expanded later to include several other lawyers.

He wrote a full-length play "Climate of Fear," which was produced by the Raleigh Little Theatre in 1954. The play dealt with the evils of McCarthyism. With his father Clarence, he wrote a book titled *Poe-Pourri, A North Carolina Cavalcade*. He was active in civic affairs, e.g., the Wake County Bar Association, the NCSU Friends of the Library, and the Watauga Club. He was a golfer, tennis player, and a bridge master.

Charlie married in 1939 the former Betty Shigley, with whom he had three children, Betsy Sharp, Mary Twitchell, and Charles A. Poe, Jr. Charlie and Betty also had seven grandchildren.

Charles Poe died in Raleigh on July 22, 1994.[28]

RALPH FADUM

Ralph Eigel Fadum was born in Pittsburgh, Pennsylvania, on July 19, 1912. He received his bachelor's degree in civil engineering from the University of Illinois and his master's and doctoral degrees in soil

---

North Carolina Press, 1979.

[28] Adapted from eulogy of Charles Poe by Joseph Cheshire, Jr., unpublished, December 13, 1994, Sandwich Club files.

mechanics and foundation engineering from Harvard University. He taught at Harvard and Purdue University before joining N.C. State's faculty. Purdue awarded him an honorary doctorate of engineering in 1963.

An international authority in the field of geotechnical engineering, he served as Dean of Engineering from 1962 to 1978. Prior to that, he served as head of the Department of Civil Engineering from 1949-1962. He was also designated as Professor Emeritus of Civil Engineering.

Dean Fadum's first wife was Nancy Fadum, one of the first female attorneys in Raleigh. Their house next to the Carolina Country Club was of modern design. Fadum married a second time, to Elaine Lawrence.

Throughout his career, his contributions had considerable impact on national goals of engineering education and the engineering profession, as well as on his students and colleagues. He was an energetic advocate of programs that opened the engineering profession to many more women and minorities. His distinguished record in supporting excellence in engineering education and his pioneering work in soil mechanics and foundation engineering were recognized in 1975 by his election to the National Academy of Engineering, the highest distinction conferred on an engineer.

As engineering dean, he was instrumental in the development of important programs and centers devoted to special technologies, including the Center for Acoustical Studies, the Center for Marine and Coastal Studies, the Engineering Design Center, the Engineer-in-Residence Program, the Productivity Research and Extension Program (which evolved into the Integrated Manufacturing Engineering Systems Institute), the Water Resources Research Institute and the Furniture Research and Development Applications Institute.

As a leader in the areas of soil mechanics and foundation engineering, his expertise was sought by the Department of Defense, the Department of the Army, the Department of the Air Force, the National Science Foundation and the U.S. Department of Transportation. He worked on many projects, including the Trans-Alaska pipeline, the permafrost study in Greenland and the NASA Apollo program launching facilities.

Dr. Fadum belonged to numerous scientific, professional and honorary societies and was a Fellow of the American Society of Civil Engineers. His honors and awards included the Department of the Army's Outstanding Civilian Service Medal, Outstanding Civil Engineer in North Carolina and the Award of Merit from the N.C. State University Alumni Association. In 1995, he was awarded the Holladay Medal for Excellence by the N.C. State Board of Trustees in recognition of his outstanding career. In April of 2000 he was designated a Fellow of the Professional Engineers of North Carolina.

As a champion of athletics, Dr. Fadum served as chairman of N.C. State's Faculty Athletics Committee (1961-1973), as president of the Atlantic Coast Conference (1966-1969 and 1971-1972) and as a member of the Council of the National Athletics Association (1972-1976).

Dr. Fadum, Dean Emeritus of N.C. State's College of Engineering, died July 12, 2000. He was survived by his wife, Elaine Lawrence Fadum; a daughter, Jane Fields Fadum of Raleigh; a brother, Torgier B. Fadum, Jr., and his wife, Mary, of Grand Island, New York; two stepdaughters, Cynthia Haverly of Valparaiso, Indiana, and Linda Eason of Canton, Michigan; and a step-granddaughter, Kristen Eason. Dr. Fadum was predeceased by a brother, Hans Fadum and a sister, Mildrid Brown.[29]

HAL TRENTMAN

W. Hal Trentman was born in 1897 in Adams, Nebraska, on a wheat and stock farm. In the summer of 1917 he worked at an inn in Colorado owned by the naturalist Enos A. Mills, who had a strong influence on Hal's thinking.

He served in the U.S. Cavalry in 1918 but did not get to the European front of World War I. After the war he took a job with the New Mexico Agricultural Service.

Hal came to Raleigh in 1926 as an employee of Occidental Life Insurance Co. He rose to the post of executive vice president, president, and chairman of the board before retiring in 1962. During that period he was a member of the Raleigh-Durham Airport Authority for 17 years.

He ran successfully for Wake County commissioner and held the post for eight years, until 1970. He served as chairman the last six years. His participation in county government was marked by unusually good cooperation among the commissioners. He had the ability to make people feel at ease. In 1971 he was selected by the *News & Observer* as Tar Heel of the Week.

In later years Hal lived on a farm in Neuse Township with his wife. They had two daughters, Jean Marie and Betty.[30]

---

[29] Adapted from obituary, *NC State Engineering News,* Summer 2000, http://www.engr.ncsu.edu/news/awards/awards.arc.00.summer.html, accessed 10 May 2010.

[30] Adapted from *News and Observer*, Raleigh, North Carolina, January 9, 1970; February 14, 1971. Courtesy of the Elizabeth Reid Murray Collection, Olivia

DR. CHAUNCEY ROYSTER

Dr. Chauncey L. Royster was born around 1910. He attended the University of North Carolina at Chapel Hill, according to the publication *Yackety Yak* where he was listed as a freshman in 1928. He received a letter for basketball in 1931.

He earned the degree Doctor of Medicine and became Associate Physician at Rex Hospital in Raleigh. He engaged in medical research and published a paper in 1942 titled "Potential Health Hazards in a Changing Social and Economic World" at a conference of the American College of Physicians. Another paper was "Blood Pressure and Sulfocyanates" in the *American Journal of the Medical Sciences*.

Dr. Chauncey Royster was president of the Wake County Medical Society in 1968.

While watching Professor Bill Sonner of North Carolina State University teach swimming endurance to children Dr. Royster had the idea of applying the methods to middle-aged men. In the Fall of 1961 he initiated a Men's Physical Fitness Program involving calisthenics and later jogging. The result was very successful and served to stimulate such activities widely. In 1973 he reported the findings in the *British Journal of Sports Medicine* in a paper, "Training at Different Ages."

An article about the program appeared in *The Leader*, the Research Triangle Newsweekly, for May 31, 1979.[31]

CHARLES ARTHUR

Charles Davis (Zack) Arthur was born October 25, 1900, in Raleigh. He was the son of a seafood dealer and had three brothers. His nickname "Zack" was given him as a child, for an unknown reason. He entered North Carolina State College in 1917, earning a B.S. in Chemical Engineering in 1921 and another B.S. in Civil Engineering in 1924.

His first job was with the State Highway Commission. Soon

Raney Local History Library, Raleigh, North Carolina.
[31] Jones, Gloria, "For your body, try the NCSU program," *The Leader*, Year 13, Number 37, Research Triangle Park, N.C., May 31, 1979; N.C. State Physical Education website, www.ncsu.edu/pe/adultfitness/history.html, accessed 20 October 2009.

afterward he became a fire inspector for manufacturing plants, an activity lasting from 1925 to 1940. One of the organizations he worked for was Great American Insurance Company. There he progressed in his knowledge and capability in administration.

After a five-year stay in New York, he was offered and accepted in 1947 a position in Raleigh. He became manager of Great American for the Carolinas and Virginia, retiring in 1967.

By virtue of the breadth of Zack Arthur's interests and activities, he qualified as a renaissance man.

He was a dedicated parent. He married the former Anna Ball Thomas in 1931. They had two daughters—Anna Ball Mayo of Little Washington and Elizabeth High (later Bell) of Fayetteville and Raleigh. Zack introduced the girls to literature and the arts.

Zack was an avid reader, visiting the local library to take out books, mainly on military history, his special interest. He often ordered books from England. He initiated discussion of his reading with the family during dinner. He was a member of the board of the Wake County Libraries. A generous memorial endowment in his name was set up for the North Carolina State Libraries. His daughter Elizabeth has been a principal contributor to the endowment. Funds received have permitted the acquisition of hundreds of books. Zack spent much time and effort in behalf of historic preservation. He was on the board of the Raleigh Historic Properties Commission. One of his hobbies was the design and construction of model vintage ships.

Arthur was president of the Raleigh Cemetery Association, which is non-profit organization created in 1869 that oversees Oakwood Cemetery. Oakwood is the resting place of thousands of Confederate soldiers, generals, governors, and North Carolina Supreme Court justices.

Zack served as consultant to legislative study commissions on insurance matters. He was a loyal fan of the athletic program of his alma mater, attending practices and football games regularly. He was recognized by the *News & Observer* as Tar Heel of the Week October 26, 1975, the day after his 75th birthday.

Of special interest to the readers of this biography is Zack's dedication to the Sandwich Club of Raleigh. He served as able chairman of that group for more than 20 years. He gave a number of memorable talks on history over that period. Members of the club recall him as modest, kindly, courtly, and affable as well as a true intellectual.

Charles (Zack) Arthur died January 21, 1992.[32]

---

[32] Adapted from biographical material supplied by Elizabeth Arthur Bell; Christian, Kathleen, "Acres of Souls," *The Leader*, August 24, 1989.

RAYMOND L. MURRAY

Raymond Murray was a native of Nebraska. He received his bachelors and masters degrees from the University of Nebraska, studied under J. Robert Oppenheimer at the University of California, and received the doctors degree in physics at the University of Tennessee. He is a member of Phi Beta Kappa, Sigma Xi, and is a Fellow of the American Nuclear Society and of the American Physical Society.

In World War II he did research at Berkeley on the electromagnetic method of uranium isotope separation and served at Oak Ridge as a supervisor in production of material for the first atomic bomb. After the war he headed service and research groups.

In 1950 he joined the Physics Department at North Carolina State College. There he helped build the first university nuclear reactor and initiate the first nuclear engineering program. He became Head of Physics in 1960. In the school year 1962-63 he visited a number of foreign countries. He served as Head of the Nuclear Engineering Department from 1963 to 1972.

At N.C. State Dr. Murray taught reactor analysis, directed graduate research, and served as consultant to industry and government. He was the author of many technical papers and several books. He received a number of honors, including the O. Max Gardner Award of North Carolina and was recognized in *Who's Who in America*.

After retirement in 1980, he was a consultant to Bechtel Corp. in the Three Mile Island recovery program and served as chairman of the group seeking unsuccessfully to establish a low-level radioactive waste disposal facility.

He was married to Ilah Mae Rengler from 1941 to 1966, to Quin Davies Meyer from 1967 to 1977, and to Elizabeth Davis Reid from 1979. He has three children—Stephen, Ilah Maureen, and Marshall, stepchildren Tucker, Michael, Nancy, and Jim, and several grandchildren and great grandchildren.

Dr. Murray joined the Sandwich Club in 1957 and was a contemporary of Charles Johnson, one of the club's founders in 1924. Dr. Murray served as chairman of the Sandwich Club for many years.[33]

---

[33] Biographical sketch supplied by Raymond L. Murray.

ALFRED T. HAMILTON

Dr. Alfred Thompson Hamilton, 80, died March 30, 1993. He was the widower of Eileen Frances O'Brien, who died in 1990.

A memorial service was held at Christ Episcopal Church. He was buried in the Old Chapel Hill Cemetery.

A native of Chapel Hill, Dr. Hamilton attended Staunton (Va.) Military Academy and received his A.B. degree from the University of North Carolina. He studied medicine at UNC for two years and went on to receive his M.D. degree from Harvard University.

He served his internship at the Roosevelt Hospital in New York City and his surgical residency at the Lahey Clinic in Boston. He was a member of the U.S. Army Medical Corps between 1941 and 1946 with service in the European Theater. He left the Army as a lieutenant colonel.

Dr. Hamilton began his private practice in Raleigh in 1946. He was on the staffs of Rex Hospital, St. Agnes, and Wake County Memorial Hospital, ultimately serving as chief of surgery and staff president of Rex, president of the Wake County Medical Society, and president of the North Carolina Surgical Association. For many years, Dr. Hamilton did general surgery at Central Prison in Raleigh, and was director at Central Prison after his active surgical practice ended.

Dr. Hamilton was a longtime member of the North Carolina Blue Cross/Blue Shield Board of Trustees. He was a member of the Southern Medical Association, the American Medical Association and the Southeastern Surgical Congress; he was a Fellow of the American College of Surgeons and a Diplomate of the American Board of Surgery.

He was a member of the Carolina Country Club, the Sandwich Club and Milburnie Fishing Club.

Surviving were sons, Alfred T. Hamilton Jr., of Chicago, Ill., Hugh de Roulhac Hamilton of Chesapeake, Va, Daniel Heyward Hamilton and James Stephen Hamilton, both of Raleigh; and five grandchildren. Dr. Hamilton's late father, Dr. J. G. de Roulhac Hamilton, was a renowned historian at UNC-Chapel Hill and the founder of the Southern Historical Collection.[34]

---

[34] Adapted from obituary, *News and Observer*, Raleigh, North Carolina, March 31, 1993. Courtesy of Elizabeth Reid Murray Collection, Olivia Raney Local History Library, Raleigh, North Carolina.

GAYLORD NOYCE

Gaylord Brewster Noyce '52 M.Div., professor emeritus of the practice of pastoral theology at Yale Divinity School, died Aug. 10, 2009, at home in Hamden, CT, at the age of 83, after a quarter-century struggle with Parkinson's disease.

An industrious author who helped train generations of future church leaders during his 34 years at YDS, Noyce devoted his considerable energy as a writer and teacher to pastoral issues.

"His focus was always on the church and how the church could function more effectively in the current world," recalled Horace Bushnell Professor Emeritus of Christian Nurture Harry Adams, whose tenure at YDS as professor and dean overlapped with Noyce's. "His books are all focused on ministry and parish and church. That was the main focus of his intellectual life and his professional life."

The son of a Congregational minister, Noyce grew up in Iowa, graduating as the valedictorian of Grinnell High School. Following completion of a wartime stint in the U.S. Navy and a mathematics degree from Miami University in Ohio, Noyce in 1949 moved to New Haven with his new wife, Dorothy, to enroll at YDS.

Noyce's graduating class, the Class of 1952, went on to become a powerhouse of loyalty and generosity to YDS. In 2007, at its 55th reunion, the Class of 1952 honored Noyce with an evening buffet at a New Haven hotel. It included a fond tribute by Rev. Samuel Slie '52 M.Div., '63 S.T.M. In his 20-minute talk, Slie described how Noyce appeared upon entering YDS in 1949: "Very good looking, not much weight, rather slight and yet he was to be an amazing person among us all." Slie and Noyce's careers overlapped repeatedly in the decades following graduation. Through it all, Slie recalled recently, "He was just a wonderful person, always. He was deeply committed. He was good with colleagues."

After graduating from YDS, Noyce served Congregational churches in Lexington, Massachusetts, and Raleigh, North Carolina, but, by 1960, had answered a call by then dean Liston Pope to return to YDS as an assistant professor of pastoral theology and to run the field education program that gave students practical experience. Judging by a host of administrative appointments at YDS that came in the following years, Noyce fit in well as he assisted with Berkeley Divinity School's merger with YDS and became YDS's first dean of students. Another indication of Noyce's quick acceptance to the YDS community came in the spring of 1961, when the YDS faculty raised $1,000 to bail Noyce out of an

Alabama jail, where he had landed as part of a Freedom Ride drawing attention to racial segregation in the American South.

As a teacher and mentor, Noyce drew on these experiences to impart the grit and flavor of pastoral work to students who were not necessarily sufficiently seasoned to fully grasp it. Kristen Leslie '86 M.Div. was one of those students. "Trying to understand the realities of ministry could be very difficult for someone who didn't have much life experience," said Leslie, who was 25 when she graduated and is now an associate professor of pastoral care and counseling at YDS. "His teaching came out of a place of experience. He understood the ambiguities of working in ministry. He understood that with the richness of ministry always come complications."

The titles of Noyce's 11 books reflect this commitment to exploring pastoral issues and nuances: *The Church is Not Expendable* (Westminster, 1970), *Survival and Mission for the City Church* (Westminster, 1975), and *The Minister as Moral Counselor* (Abingdon, 1989).

Off campus, Noyce steeped himself in ministry opportunities, ranging from a seven-month term as interim minister at Hamden's Spring Glen Church to serving as a leader of the EXIT coffeehouse outreach effort on the New Haven Green and traveling as a delegate to United Church of Christ synods across the country. With his family, Noyce was a member of the Spring Glen Church for several decades.

"There's no question that he was really, truly one of the most gracious, humble church members that any pastor could hope to have," said Spring Glen's senior pastor, Andrew Nagy-Benson '98 M.Div. "He was someone whose credentials and wisdom could let him tell you how it is, but he was always someone who asked, 'How is it?'"

After retiring in 1994 from YDS, Noyce remained connected to the school, in part through a scholarship bearing his name. Established in 1996, it benefited entering YDS students. Upon learning of Noyce's death, one such student, Stephen Ogden '09 M.A.R., wrote in a recent e-mail that the scholarship aid was "absolutely essential" to being able to attend YDS. Now a doctoral student at Yale, Ogden credited the YDS M.A.R. program with allowing him "to pursue both my passions, philosophy and theology, in a way that I do not think any other master's program in the country could."

Noyce's last visit to the Sterling Divinity Quadrangle came just weeks before his death. On a Sunday afternoon, YDS Dean Harold Attridge took Noyce, wife Dorothy Noyce and two other family members on a quickly arranged tour of the empty Quad. "Gay's last visit to YDS was a bittersweet occasion," recalled Attridge, the Reverend Henry L. Slack Dean and Lillian Claus Professor of New Testament. "Gay himself was delighted to be back at YDS, and proud to show it off to his granddaughter and her husband. It was clear that this might be his last occasion to visit, but that did not dampen his enthusiasm."

Noyce was survived by his wife of 60 years, Dorothy, along with two daughters, Betsy and Karen, and a son, Timothy.[35]

SAM RAGAN

Sam Ragan (1915-1996) was a favorite son of North Carolina whose career was spent as a journalist, author, poet and champion of the arts.

He was born in Berea, North Carolina, the son of William Samuel Ragan and Emma Clare (Long) Ragan. In 1936 he graduated from Atlantic Christian, now Barton College, in Wilson, North Carolina, and married Marjorie Usher in 1939. He served briefly as a reporter for the *San Antonio Evening News,* later known as the *San Antonio Express-News,* and then returned to North Carolina where, beginning in 1941, he held various editorial positions with the Raleigh *News & Observer.*

While with the *News & Observer* he began writing *Southern Accent,* a weekly newspaper column of literary criticism, commentary and poetry. It became the longest running column in the United States and appeared in forty-three states and twenty-four foreign countries. In 1969 he purchased *The Pilot,* a small weekly newspaper in Southern Pines, North Carolina. Ragan served as its editor and publisher, remaining active on *The Pilot's* staff until his death.

In addition to his work as a newspaperman Sam Ragan published six collections of verse including *Journey Into Morning* and *To The Water's Edge* as well as several works of non-fiction. However, he may be best known as a public intellectual and a widely admired advocate of the arts. He was the first secretary of the North Carolina Department of Cultural Resources and the first chair of the North Carolina Arts Council. He taught creative writing and journalism at Sandhills Community College, St. Andrews Presbyterian College and North Carolina State University. He served as president of the Associated Press Managing

---

[35] Adapted from obituary, "Prof. Gaylord Noyce Dies at 83," Yale Divinity School News, website http://www.yale.edu/divinity/news/090813_news_noyce.shtml accessed 19 October 2009.

Editors and the North Carolina Press Association. In addition to serving on the boards of several associations devoted to history, music and the humanities he helped found and guide the North Carolina School of the Arts, and the Weymouth Center for the Arts and Humanities.

A member of the Presbyterian church, Ragan was also a life-long champion of the Democratic Party. In addition to his many works of poetry in 1961 he wrote *The Democratic Party: Its Aims and Purposes* and with Elizebeth Ives in 1969 he wrote *Back to Beginnings: Adlai E. Stevenson and North Carolina*. North Carolina Governor Terry Sanford described Sam Ragan as "one of North Carolina's treasures. He was a crusading editorial force at the *News & Observer* where he fought for the improvement of education, the elimination of racial injustice and the broadening of economic opportunities."

Ragan was a recipient of the North Carolina Award in Fine Arts, the John Taylor Caldwell Award for The Humanities, The Roanoke-Chowan Award for Poetry, the R. Hunt Parker Award for Literary Achievement, the Morrison Award and the North Carolinian Society Award. He was elected to both the North Carolina Journalism Hall of Fame and the North Carolina Literary Hall of Fame. Ragan was awarded honorary doctorates at St. Andrews Presbyterian College in Laurinburg, North Carolina, Atlantic Christian (Barton) College, The University of North Carolina at Chapel Hill and Methodist College in Fayetteville, North Carolina. In 1982 Governor Jim Hunt named Sam Ragan North Carolina's Poet Laureate for life.

In 1981 St. Andrews Presbyterian College initiated the Sam Ragan Fine Arts Awards. These awards are given annually "in honor of Sam Ragan, North Carolina's first secretary of Cultural Resources, and to celebrate the fact that North Carolina was the first of the United States to establish a cabinet-level position recognizing the fine arts." Barton College founded the Sam and Marjorie Ragan Writing Center in their honor. In 2003 the North Carolina Literary and Historical Association paid tribute to Ragan's memory by establishing the Ragan Old North State Award Cup for Nonfiction.

Elena Ruehr composed a musical piece titled "Exodus" based on four poems by Sam Ragan. The work was commissioned by the Coastal Carolina Chamber Music Festival and premiered during the 2005 season.[36]

---

[36] Adapted from Wikipedia entry, http://en.wikipedia.org/wiki/Sam_Ragan, accessed on 19 October 2009.

ALEX B. ANDREWS

Brigadier General Alexander Boyd Andrews, III, was born in Raleigh on January 12, 1913, the son of Mabel Young and John Hawkins Andrews. His grandfather, Colonel A. B. Andrews, pioneered railroads built through western North Carolina.

After graduating from Woodberry Forest School, he received his B.A. in 1934 and L.L.B. in 1936 from the University of North Carolina in Chapel Hill, where he was editor of the annual *Yackety-Yack*, and member of Phi Beta Kappa and Sigma Alpha Epsilon. After graduate work at Northwestern Law School, Chicago, Illinois, he specialized in tax law in Chicago and New York.

Called to active duty as a Lieutenant on December 12, 1941, his military career began with learning to fly on his own, as he was 28 and overage for military flight training. Senior and Command Pilot after an overseas tour, his assignment with the Eighth Air Force in England involved classified work in combat intelligence, where he flew B-17 aircraft 60 combat hours. On one 1944 bombing mission, his B-17 Flying Fortress was badly crippled by enemy fire over Nazi-controlled France. Military protocol called for the crew to abandon the plane, but a wounded bombardier couldn't make the jump. Major Andrews crawled through the plane's mangled nose section, gave the bombardier a shot of morphine and his own oxygen mask, then nursed the plane back to England for a miraculous emergency landing. Andrews's B-17 was publicized as one of the most disabled planes ever to return to base. Author John Hersey used Andrews's personal recount of that mission in his book *The War Lover* (1959), which was made into a movie in 1962 starring Steve McQueen, with Andrews serving as Technical Director.

Receiving the Distinguished Flying Cross and Air Medal, he was the first North Carolina reservist to qualify as a jet pilot, with 5,000 total hours; and in 1961, the first North Carolinian to be promoted to Brigadier General in the Air Force Reserve which was awarded by President John F. Kennedy. He also helped establish a practice bomb range vital to the Tactical Air Command mission. Retiring in 1973, he later served as a Director of the Eighth Air Force Association for eight years.

Alex Andrews's business pursuits were as interesting as his military life. He was a founder of eleven companies including B.T.I. (Business Telecom, Inc.), North Carolina Natural Gas Corporation and Sugar Mountain Ski Resort, helping to bring the ski industry to North

Carolina. His last enthusiasm was his 746 acre North Carolina mountain, Hanging Rock.

He served on the Board of Directors of 21 companies including British American Insurance Company, McMillan Corporation, and Family Health International. He established his Raleigh law firm of Mitchiner, Andrews and Yeargan; and later was Of Counsel to Jordan, Price, Wall, Gray and Jones.

He was Senior Warden of the Church of the Good Shepherd and a director of numerous civic and charitable organizations including the Wake County Cancer Society, Greater Raleigh United Fund, Heart Fund, Chamber of Commerce and Rotary Club.

He was a member of the N.C. Society of the Cincinnati, Carolina Country Club, Circle Club, Capital Cotillion Club, Sphinx Club and Terpsichorean Club of Raleigh, and the Coral Bay Club at Atlantic Beach.

Alex Andrews died on March 7, 1999. He was survived by his wife of 25 years, Marti Rose Andrews; daughter Mabel Cook of Charlotte; sons, Alex B. "Andy" Andrews, IV, George H. Andrews of Raleigh; and six grandchildren, Edward, Drew and William Cook, Rhyne and Alex Andrews, and Ashley James Andrews. He was preceded in death by his son, James Rose Andrews.[37]

JAMES CURRIE

James S. Currie was born March 17, 1919, in Clarkton in Bladen County. He graduated from Davidson College and received additional degrees from UNC at Chapel Hill.

In 1941 Currie joined the Federal Housing Authority in Greensboro and later combined the practice of law in Chapel Hill with teaching business law at the university.

Governor Kerr Scott appointed Currie tax research director for the state in 1950. He also served as executive secretary for the State Tax Study Commission, which developed major changes in the tax structure of the state.

Governor Luther Hodges selected James Currie to be the state's Commissioner of Revenue in 1957. He held that post until 1961, when he joined Carolina Power and Light as assistant treasurer. He became

---

[37] Adapted from obituary, *News and Observer*, Raleigh, North Carolina, March 8, 1999. Courtesy of the Olivia Raney Local History Library, Raleigh, North Carolina. "A War Hero's Story," *The Rotarian*, April 2000, Vol. 176, No. 4, p. 31.

treasurer of CP&L in 1967.

He took early retirement in 1978 and under Governor James Hunt became the state's Commissioner of Banks, as head of the State Banking Commission.

James was married to the former Virginia Spruill of Plymouth. They had two children. He died July 25, 1991, at the age of 72.[38]

HARRY GATTON

Thomas Harry Gatton of 501 East Whitaker Mill Road in Raleigh died Saturday, July 28, 2001.

Born March 10, 1918, in Harmony, Iredell County, N.C., he was the son of the late Thomas Lee and Freddie Moore Gatton.

Gatton, who was known as Harry, graduated from the University of North Carolina at Chapel Hill and was a member of the Order of the Golden Fleece. He was a World War II veteran, U.S. Navy Lt. Commander. Gatton married Mary Gordon of Detroit, Michigan, September 12, 1942. He was also a former newspaper editor and radio station director.

In the 1950s Gatton served as Administrative Assistant to U.S. Senator Alton Lennon (N.C.) and Executive Secretary to U.S. Senator Sam J. Ervin, Jr. (N.C.). From 1960 to 1981 he was Executive Vice President of the N.C. Bankers Association. Bank Historian and author of ten published state banking histories, he was former Chairman of the Board, School of Banking of the South at Louisiana State University; former member of the Board of Directors of the American Bankers Association; and member of the Presidential Advisory Board of Campbell University where he was awarded honorary Doctor of Law Degree. The T. Harry Gatton Trust Scholarship was named for him at Campbell University. Former member of the Board, Peace College, and former member of the Board, N.C. State University, Humanities Foundation, Gatton was accredited professionally as a Certified Association Executive. As an active member of Hayes Barton United Methodist Church, he served as Chairman of the Administrative Board and Board of Trustees. He was a former member of the Board of Directors of the Methodist Homes, Inc., Durham. Gatton was a Past President of the Rotary Club of Raleigh and a Paul Harris Fellow. Member for 14 years of the American Battle Monuments Commission, Gatton served as former Chairman of the North Carolina Historical

---

[38] Adapted in part from *News and Observer*, Raleigh, North Carolina, August 9, 1957; September 17, 1957; August 2, 1978. Courtesy of North Carolina Collection, University of North Carolina, Chapel Hill, North Carolina.

Commission, was awarded the Christopher Crittenden cup for the preservation of N.C. history, and was a member of the U.S. Bicentennial Council of the 13 Original States. He was designated Tar Heel of the Week in 1969 by the Raleigh *News and Observer* and was a member of the Carolina Country Club.

Mr. Gatton was preceded in death by a brother, James Gatton, and a sister, Marie G. Myers.

In addition to his wife Mary, survivors included: brothers, Frank Gatton of Raleigh, Clarence Gatton of Falls Church, VA., Clyde Gilmore of Greensboro, N.C.; nieces, Jan G. Kalmus of Crofton, MD, and Mary Ann Gatton of Centerville, VA; and nephews, Steven Gatton of Statesville, N.C., John Gatton of Raleigh, Kevin Gatton of Mt. Pleasant, S.C., David Gatton of Culpepper, VA, James Myers and Bobby Gilmore of Greensboro, N.C., and Tom Gatton of Houston, TX.[39]

WILLIAM SPRUNT III

William Sprunt III was a graduate of Davidson College in 1942. He served in the U.S. Navy during World War II.

He earned his M.D. from Harvard Medical School in 1945, specializing in radiology. In 1961, he moved to Raleigh to start a partnership in radiology at Wake Medical Center with Dr. Albert M. Jenkins. The partnership grew to become Wake Radiology, employing over fifty-eight radiologists. Offices were established in Raleigh, Cary, Garner, and Chapel Hill. Facilities that he introduced included x-rays, computed tomography and magnetic resonance imaging. The practice included both diagnosis and therapy. The practice also had a strong relationship with WakeMed hospital. Jenkins gave credit to his partner: "The radiology department at WakeMed truly is the creation of Bill Sprunt, and it continues to flourish because of the excellent staff he was able to attract."

Sprunt retired to Florida in 1997. He was active in the West Volusia Family YMCA. He was a member of the Sigma Alpha Epsilon fraternity.

Dr. Sprunt died March 20, 2007, in DeLand, Florida. Survivors included his wife, Priscilla; one son, William, Jr., of Boone, N.C.; two daughters, Suze Peace of DeLand and Martha Landt of Hilo, Hawaii; two

---

[39] Adapted from obituary, *News and Observer*, Raleigh, North Carolina, July 29, 2001, Sandwich Club files.

sisters, Edna Mitchell of Winston-Salem, N.C., and Nancy Mathes of Memphis, Tenn.; seven grandchildren and four great-grandchildren.[40]

RUFFIN BAILEY

J. Ruffin Bailey was born in 1919 in Onslow County. His father was prominent lawyer I. M. Bailey and his mother was the former Ida Thompson. The family moved to Raleigh when Ruffin was six years old. He attended public schools, then UNC at Chapel Hill, where he graduated in 1941.

He joined the Army Air Corps as a pilot, and flew "over the hump" in the Asian war theater. For that he was awarded the Air Medal and the Distinguished Flying Cross.

Ruffin returned to UNC and received a law degree in 1948. That post-war class was close-knit and each was able to assist their classmates. On graduation the young Bailey took a job as a law clerk, but soon became a member of a firm established by his father. Wright T. Dixon, Jr., became a partner in the company.

I. M. Bailey served as mentor and adviser to his son, instilling high standards in Ruffin.

Ruffin married the former Nelle Rousseau of North Wilkesboro, N.C. They had two children.

In 1964, at age 44, Ruffin ran for the State Senate. Successful, he served four terms in the General Assembly, from 1965 to 1973. He was chairman of several important committees. After his legislative service he became a highly respected lobbyist, well-known for his integrity and credibility. Those qualities led to his receipt of the 2001 Joseph Branch Professional Award, the highest law honor in Wake County.

J. Ruffin Bailey died in 2006.[41]

---

[40] "History of Wake Radiology," Albert M. Jenkins, M.D., FACR, and "Our History," http://www.wakerad.com/about-wr/history/, accessed 10 January 2010 and 31 January 2011; Davidson College, Class Memorials, Summer 2010, http://www3.davidson.edu/cms/x24892.xml, accessed 10 January 2010.
[41] Adapted from *News and Observer*, Raleigh, North Carolina, January 17, 1964, Courtesy of North Carolina Collection, University of North Carolina, Chapel Hill; "History of Bailey & Dixon, L.L.P.," http://www.bdixon.com/history/, accessed 7 May 2010.

EDWARD RANKIN

Edward Lee Rankin, Jr., was born May 12, 1919, in Chattanooga, TN, the son of E. L. Rankin and Gladys Narramore Rankin. His youth was spent in Spencer, N.C. In the fall of 1936 he entered the University of North Carolina and worked his way through college. He was very active in connection with the student newspaper the *Daily Tar Heel*. He received his A.B. degree in Journalism.

After a brief stay as reporter with the Salisbury *Evening Post* and the Raleigh *News & Observer*, Edward enlisted in the U.S. Navy in October 1941. He was assigned to Landing Ship, Tank LST 356, which invaded in Sicily and Salerno and invaded Normandy on D-day. He was en route to Hawaii when the war with Japan ended. He was lieutenant commander when his active duty ended.

On return, he became associated with Governor William Umstead and became his private secretary. Later he was private secretary to Governor Luther Hodges and had the distinction of serving two governors.

Edward was married to the former Frances Wallace, with whom he had two daughters. He was a member of Pullen Memorial Baptist Church and was active in government and civic affairs. He served in 1982 as president of the UNC General Alumni Association (the first president was John Motley Morehead, 1843-1849). He was a charter member of the North Caroliniana Society. Edward Lee Rankin, Jr., died in 2006.[42]

JACOB KOOMEN

Dr. Jacob Koomen, Jr., was born in 1917 in Bristol, New York. As a youth he lived on a farm and attended a one-room country school. He entered the University of Rochester in 1935 and on graduation in 1939 began study in the School of Medicine, receiving his degree in 1945.

In 1943 Koomen married the former Ruth Chapin of Canandaigua, NY. They had four children—Scotty, Marcia, Nancy, and Neil.

From 1946 to 1954 he taught at the medical school, then joined the U.S. Public Health Service, with assignment to North Carolina. He soon

---

[42] Adapted from "Tar Heel of the Week: Edward L. Rankins, Jr.," *News and Observer*, Raleigh, North Carolina, January 2, 1955, Courtesy of North Carolina Collection, University of North Carolina, Chapel Hill, North Carolina.

switched to working for the State of North Carolina. His specialty was epidemiology, the study of communicable diseases like diphtheria, typhoid fever, and hepatitis. From a position that emphasized epidemiology he became Assistant Director of the state Health Department and eventually Director, in 1966. During his tenure, he worked to make childhood vaccinations mandatory and also helped establish a state medical examiner system.

In 1960 Koomen received the Reynolds Award from the N.C. Public Health Association. In 1961 he was named Tar Heel of the Week by the *News & Observer*. He was a trustee of the University of Rochester.

In 1978 Dr. Koomen resigned as chief health officer to take a teaching position at the University of North Carolina at Chapel Hill in the School of Public Health. He retired from that job in the early 1980s.

Jake Koomen was famous in the Sandwich Club for his detailed talks on common objects and for the wealth of information that he possessed.

He died in 2006 at the age of 88.[43]

RALPH REEVES

Ralph Bernard Reeves, Jr., was born in 1920 in Brunswick, Georgia. He entered N.C. State College at the age of 15 and graduated in 1941 with a B.S. in Architectural Engineering. In college he was a classmate of architect F. Carter Williams and a close associate of future UNC President William Friday. In later years Reeves and Friday cooperated on plans for various buildings.

After graduation he joined the U.S. Army and served as captain, receiving several medals for his outstanding service in the Pacific theater.

In 1948 he formed a partnership with John Holloway that lasted 36 years. He provided architectural leadership for many buildings, including the North Carolina Museum of Art, the North Carolina Legislative Building, the Wake Medical Center, and the Wake County Courthouse.

The firm of Holloway and Reeves of which he was president provided design services for 30 major hospitals, 40 public and private schools, and 100 churches, banks, and prisons.

---

[43] Adapted from "Tar Heel of the Week: Dr. Jacob Koomen," *News and Observer*, Raleigh, North Carolina, October 22, 1961; *News and Observer,* September 9, 1978, Courtesy of North Carolina Collection, University of North Carolina, Chapel Hill, North Carolina; "In Memoriam," *Rochester Review,* Fall 2006, Vol. 69, No. 1.

Ralph was recognized in 1963 by the *News & Observer* as Tar Heel of the Week. He was a member of the American Institute of Architects and a member of the Carolina Country Club.

He was survived by his wife, Frances Campbell ("Cam") Reeves; son Ralph Bernard Reeves, III, a Raleigh publisher; son Ross Campbell Reeves of Norfolk, Virginia; a brother, Col. Owen T. Reeves of Santa Rosa, California; and several grandchildren.

Ralph Reeves died at the early age of 63 on May 12, 1984, at his home at 815 Marlowe Road.[44]

DR. H. G. JONES

Dr. Houston Gwynne Jones, born in 1924 on a tenant farm in Caswell County, received his undergraduate training at Appalachian State Teachers College, master's degree from George Peabody College, and PhD from Duke University.

During World War II, he served as a Sonarman in the Navy's anti-submarine warfare in the Mediterranean, participating in the invasions of Anzio and Southern France, and anti-mine warfare in the China Sea, preparing for the planned invasion of Japan. After attending college on the G.I. Bill, he began his career as a history teacher in colleges in North Carolina and Georgia. From 1956 to 1968 he was State Archivist of North Carolina and, from 1968 to 1974, Director of the State Department of Archives and History. For the next twenty years he was Director of the North Carolina Collection and Adjunct Professor of History at the University of North Carolina at Chapel Hill. Upon semi-retirement, he continued as Thomas Whitmell Davis Research Historian at the UNC-CH Library.

Dr. Jones served as President of the Society of American Archivists, Secretary of the American Association for State and Local History, Secretary of the Joint Committee on the Status of the National Archives, Commissioner of the National Historical Publications and Records Commission, Chairman of America's Four Hundredth Anniversary Committee, President of the North Carolina Literary and Historical Association, and Commissioner of the North Carolina Historical Commission. He was the recipient of SAA's Waldo Leland Prize,

---

[44] Adapted from obituary, *News and Observer*, Raleigh, North Carolina, May 13, 1964, Courtesy of North Carolina Collection, University of North Carolina, Chapel Hill, North Carolina.

AASLH's Award of Distinction, NHPRC's Award for Distinguished Service in Documentary Publication and Preservation, NCL&HA's Christopher Crittenden Award, John Tyler Caldwell Award for lifetime services to the humanities, and the North Carolina Award, the state's highest honor for public service.   In 1975 he founded the North Caroliniana Society and remained its unsalaried secretary for thirty-five years.

Among his books, three—*For History's Sake* (UNC Press), *North Carolina Illustrated* (UNC Press), and *Local Government Records* (AASLH)—won national awards, and a fourth—*The Records of a Nation* (Atheneum)—was used as evidence in the Nixon Presidential Records case.   Other books included *North Carolina History: An Annotated Bibliography* (Greenwood), *Sketches in North Carolina USA 1872 to 1878* (North Caroliniana Society), and *Scoundrels, Rogues and Heroes of the Old North State* (History Press). His latest publication, *The Sonarman's War* (McFarland), is his detailed account of his experience in World War II with service in Italy and the South Pacific. For seventeen years he wrote for the Associated Press the unpaid weekly article, "In Light of History," which, when he gave it up in 1986, was the longest-running syndicated state historical column in the nation.

Although his professional career was spent in "southern" history, for more than thirty-five years and fifty trips to the Arctic, Dr. Jones's avocation was studying the history and culture of the world's northernmost people, the Inuit (Eskimos). That interest was highlighted by exhibitions from his extensive Inuit Art Collection at the Ackland Art Museum, Duke University Museum of Art, North Carolina State University Crafts Center, Appalachian State University Museum, the Cultural Center of the International Development Bank, and the Winnipeg Art Gallery.[45]

JOHN V. HUNTER III

John Hunter III, born in 1930, was raised in Winston-Salem. He received his B.S. from Davidson College and his J.D. from the Law School at UNC in Chapel Hill in the 1950s. There he served as Editor in Chief of *Yackety Yak*.

In World War II he was a trial observer for the Army in France for two years. He started practicing law in 1962 and established a law office at 3105 Glenwood Ave. John also served as chair of the Young Lawyers

---

[45] Biographical sketch supplied by Dr. H. G. Jones.

Division of the North Carolina Bar Association from 1966 to 1967.

John had been interested in Russia and its political system and culture. He visited there for 10 days. He was struck by the friendliness of the Russian people, in spite of the Cold War. An extensive article about his observations in Russia appeared in the *News & Observer* on Sunday, February 16, 1964. He was elected president of the Raleigh chapter of the United Nations Association of the USA, an organization dedicated to security, human rights, and environmental protection.

John is currently retired from his law practice at Bode, Call and Stroupe, L.L.P., where he has specialized in civil litigation and land use law.[46]

MICOU BROWNE

Micou Farrar Browne was born in Raleigh in 1916. His parents were Martha Micou Farrar of Culpepper, Va., and Dr. T. E. Browne, Dean of the School of Education of North Carolina State College.

"Cou" Browne graduated with honors from N.C. State in 1936 with a business administration degree. He was employed as a clerk by Occidental Life Insurance Co. and worked his way up through Manager for Piedmont Carolina to executive vice president and president in 1962.

His progress was interrupted by World War II. As amphibious engineer he rose to rank of major and was awarded the Legion of Merit. He had served in campaigns of North Africa, Sicily, Salerno, and Normandy on D-Day.

In 1968 he resigned from Occidental and joined Durham Life Insurance Co. as executive vice president for planning. While he was in that new position a more aggressive sales policy was adopted.

Micou was married in 1938 to the former Katherine Metcalf. They he had a son Micou Metcalf Browne and a daughter Martha Lu Browne.

He was a long term member of the Kiwanis Club and the Carolina Country Club. He was very active in civic affairs, as chairman of the Raleigh Chamber of Commerce, chairman of the governor's study commission, and member of the board of trustees of Peace College.

Micou Browne died July 15, 2001.[47]

---

[46] Adapted from *News and Observer*, Raleigh, North Carolina, February 16, 1964, Courtesy of North Carolina Collection, University of North Carolina, Chapel Hill, North Carolina.

[47] Adapted from *News and Observer*, Raleigh, North Carolina, February 12, 1967, October 22, 1968, Courtesy of North Carolina Collection, University of North

HARLAN BOYLES

Harlan Edward Boyles was born May 6, 1929, in Vale, North Carolina. His father was a farmer and owner of a country store. At age 15 Harlan contracted polio that left him partially crippled.

He attended the University of Georgia briefly, but graduated in 1951 from the University of North Carolina at Chapel Hill with a major in accounting.

Harlan held several positions in state government starting in 1951. In 1960 he became Deputy Treasurer of North Carolina. As such, he assisted Edwin Gill, who was elected as State Treasurer for five four-year terms.

Boyles first ran for election in 1976 and became State Treasurer in 1977. He was re-elected several times, serving as Treasurer for 24 years until his retirement in 2001. He was highly regarded as an able and trustworthy custodian of the State's funds and as a wise advisor to the governor and the general assembly. His conservative approach assured maintenance of AAA credit rating for the state and saved taxpayers millions of dollars.

He received numerous honors, including the Distinguished Alumnus Award of UNC. He was recognized by the *News & Observer* as Tar Heel of the Week in 1975.

Harlan was married to the former Mary Frances Wilder. They had three children—Mrs. G. E. Ferrell, Frances Lynn, and Harlan, Jr.

Harlan Boyles died January 23, 2003.[48]

FRANK PARKER

Francis (Frank) Marion Parker, a Buncombe County native, was the son of Haywood and Josie Patton Parker. He was born on August 25, 1912.

Carolina, Chapel Hill, North Carolina.

[48] Adapted from "Tar Heel of the Week: There's a Bond Between the Man and His Job," *News and Observer*, Raleigh, North Carolina, June 15, 1975, Courtesy of North Carolina Collection, University of North Carolina, Chapel Hill, North Carolina; "Former Treasurer Boyles Dies," *Triangle Business Journal*, January 23, 2003.

Parker attended Asheville City schools before going on to the University of North Carolina, where he received an A.B. degree in 1934 and a law degree in 1936, graduating with honors.

In 1936, Frank Parker joined his father's Asheville law practice, which was the predecessor to today's firm McGuire, Wood and Bissette.

He served in the U.S. Army as a sergeant at the end of World War II, from 1944 to 1945.

Parker had many professional affiliations. He was a member of the North Carolina State Bar, the North Carolina Bar Association, the American Bar Association, the American Judicature Society, Phi Kappa Sigma, Phi Delta Phi, Phi Beta Kappa (1933), and the Order of the Coif (1936).

Parker was state senator for Buncombe County in the 1947 and 1949 sessions. In his first term he was chairman of trustees of the Greater University of North Carolina; in his second term he was chairman of the Wildlife Resources Committee. He was a member of several other committees.

In 1967, Parker was appointed Judge of Court of Appeals by Governor Dan K. Moore. He was then elected to the post in 1968 and remained there until 1980.

Frank Parker was appointed trustee of poet Carl Sandburg's family trust by Sandburg himself. After serving as Tribal Attorney for the Cherokee Indians for 25 years, he was made an honorary member of the Eastern Band of the Cherokee Tribe. He was also a charter member of the North Caroliniana Society. He was a lifelong member of the Trinity Episcopal Church, avid tennis player and violinist.

Judge Parker was married to the former Dorothy Acee of Asheville, with whom he had four children: Dr. Martha Elizabeth "Betsy" Parker, Dorothy Patton "Pat" Parker Peak, Mary T. Parker McAuliffe, and Frank M. Parker, Jr. Frank and Dorothy had three grandchildren: Kala Parker, Elizabeth Rhinehardt, and Jamey McAuliffe.

Frank M. Parker died in 1995 at his family home.[49]

---

[49] Adapted from *News and Observer*, Raleigh, North Carolina, January 25, 1950, December 24, 1967, January 24, 1968, Courtesy of North Carolina Collection, University of North Carolina, Chapel Hill, North Carolina; "Deaths/Funerals," *Asheville Citizen-Times*, May 17, 1995; information supplied by Richard A. Kort, attorney, McGuire, Wood & Bissette, P.A.; www.mwbavl.com accessed 28 September 2010.

WILLIAM L. WILSON

William Lenoir Wilson, MD, Brigadier General, U.S. Army (RET), died Saturday, June 6, 1998, at the age of 96.

"Blackie" Wilson was born in McGregor, TX, January 27, 1902, graduated from SMU in 1923 and attended Baylor Medical School, then in Dallas, graduating in 1926. Entering the U.S. Army Medical Corps as an ROTC graduate, he interned at Beaumont General Hospital in El Paso, TX, from 1926 to 1927. After serving 30 years in the Regular Army, he retired in 1956. Stateside assignments carried him to Iowa, Hawaii (1931-33), Colorado, Nebraska, Brooklyn, NY and Washington, DC (1935-1943). During World War II, he served in the Surgeon General's office as a Staff Officer, War Department General Staff, until mid-1943, when he completed a staff survey in the Southwest Pacific, returning for further duty in Washington.

From May 1944 to September 1946, he served in General Eisenhower's SHAEF headquarters in England, and then moved into France and finally Germany as the war ended. The then Colonel Wilson was assigned to the Office of Military Government, U.S. Zone, assuming responsibility for planning and implementing the Civilian Health Services for the German population during the Occupation. He returned to duty in Washington in late 1946. Next, Colonel Wilson served in Turkey in 1947, using his background in civilian medical care to support the Truman Four Point Program, returning from that assignment to obtain his Doctor of Public Health from Johns Hopkins University. He was on loan from the Army to the Federal Civil Defense Administration as the First Deputy Director, 1950-1953. It was during his duty at FCDA that he was promoted within the Army to Brigadier General. When he returned to Germany in 1953, it was as Seventh Army Surgeon for General A. C. Tony "Nuts" McAuliffe, his Army War College classmate in 1940. He closed out his military career as Magidan Army Hospital Commanding General in Tacoma, WA. Among his military awards is the one for which he had the greatest pride, the Typhus Commission Medal. This work contributed significantly to the prevention of that disease's outbreak amongst our troops during the War. He also received the Legion of Merit. Retiring to Austin, TX, Dr. Wilson worked for the Texas State Health Department, establishing the state's occupational and radiological health programs. In mid-1959, he moved to Raleigh at the behest of Governor Terry Sanford, and established similar programs for the N.C. Department of Health, retiring in 1969. Dr. Wilson was a past member of the Cosmos Club of Washington, D.C., the Downtown Rotary Club of Raleigh, and a member of the Raleigh Chapter of the Retired Officers' Association.

Then First Lieutenant Wilson married Frances Haywood Terry on March 23, 1927. They resided in Raleigh after Dr. Wilson's retirement, except for a brief time in Pensacola, FL, celebrating their 70th wedding anniversary 10 days before she died on April 1, 1997.

He was survived by two sons, William T. Wilson and his wife, Heidi, of El Dorado Hills, CA, and Lee H. Wilson of El Paso, TX, as well as seven grandchildren: Kerstin Wilson, Joselle Tully, Tina Wackford, Andrea Wilson, Marcella White, Christine Wilson, and Andrew Wilson. There are also seven great-grandchildren: Marielle and Holt Walker, Justine and Hunter Tully, Kendall and Andrew Wackford, and Brandy Childers.[50]

JOHN CALDWELL

John Tyler Caldwell was born December 9, 1911, in Yazoo City, Mississippi. He received a B.S. from Mississippi State College in 1932, an M.A. from Duke University in 1936, and a Ph.D. in political science from Princeton University in 1939 as a Julius Rosenwald Fellow. He was a professor of political science at Holmes Junior College in Goodman, Mississippi, from 1932 to 1936. He was a junior economist for the U.S. Resettlement Commission administration in 1936-1937 and worked in the Department of Agriculture in the summer of 1937. He was a professor of political science at Vanderbilt University from 1939 to 1947.

Caldwell entered the U.S. Navy as an Ensign in 1942 to serve in World War II and was awarded a Bronze Star for his service in the Battle of Okinawa. He left the Navy in 1946 as a Lt. Commander. Caldwell was named president of Alabama College in Montevallo, Alabama, in 1947. After leaving Montevallo in 1951, he served as president of the University of Arkansas. There, he supervised the development and expansion of the University's Graduate school and saw the beginning of the process of racial integration. This was noted by its peacefulness in contrast to problems encountered elsewhere.

In 1959 he was named chancellor of North Carolina State University, the school's eighth chief executive. During his tenure, the School of Physical Sciences and Applied Mathematics was established and

---

[50] Adapted from *News and Observer*, Raleigh, North Carolina, June 6, 1998.

the university offered degrees in the humanities and social sciences for the first time. After his retirement from the office in 1975 Caldwell continued to teach in the Department of Political Science.

At age 76 Caldwell took the position of President of Triangle Universities Center for Advanced Studies, and served from 1975 to 1982. Then he was chosen as President and CEO of the Research Triangle Foundation, overseeing the development of the Research Triangle Park.

The N.C. State Alumni Association established the John T. Caldwell Alumni Scholarship Program in 1977 to recruit outstanding high school seniors to N.C. State. These students were selected on the basis of leadership potential, outstanding scholarship, citizenship, maturity and intellectual promise. From 1977 to 2004 over 400 Caldwell Alumni Scholarships were awarded.

In 1988, the National Association of State Universities and Land-Grant Colleges named Caldwell one of Mississippi State's 10 distinguished alumni. He received honorary doctorate degrees from College of the Ozarks, Wake Forest University, and University of Maryland. The North Carolina Humanities Council named its highest honor after Caldwell. He was an Eagle Scout, recipient of the Distinguished Eagle Scout Award, and worked with Scouting much of his life.

His first wife was Helen Prentice (1942-1945). His second was the former Catherine Wadsworth Zeek, whom he married in May 1947 and with whom he had four children—Helen, Charles, Andrew, and Alice. Catherine died in 1961. His third wife was the former Carol Schroeder Erskine of Wisconsin. They were married June 1963.

Caldwell died in Raleigh, North Carolina, on October 13, 1995, at the age of 83. An editorial in *The Charlotte (N.C.) Observer* following his death stated that "the thing people remember most about John Caldwell is not how he helped build a comprehensive university and a vibrant engine of the state's economy. They remember his warmth, his affection for people, and his interest in building a decent community."[51]

BERNARD WISHY

Bernard Wishy was born in New York in 1925 and educated in the public schools there.

---

[51] Adapted from *News and Observer*, Raleigh, North Carolina, April 29, 1962, November 3, 1974, March 3, 1988, Courtesy of North Carolina Collection, University of North Carolina, Chapel Hill, North Carolina; http://en.wikipedia.org/wiki/John_Tyler_Caldwell, accessed 26 April 2010.

He served in the U.S. Army from 1942 to 1944. In 1948, he graduated from Columbia University where he majored in history. He was also named the 1948 Valedictorian for Columbia. Wishy continued his education and earned an M.A. in political science from Yale in 1949, a BLitt from Oxford in 1952, and a Ph.D. in history from Columbia in 1954. While at Columbia he was the editor of the famous Columbia series of documents about Western Civilization.

Wishy's specialty has been American and European political and intellectual history since the American Revolution. He has written or edited more than 50 books and numerous articles about those interests. Among his books are works about Thomas Jefferson, John Stuart Mill, American childhood, American family history, and a history of the American government. His book *Goodbye, Machiavelli*, published in 1997, was nominated for the Bancroft, Parkman, and Beveridge prizes in American History. Other books include: *The Child and the Republic: The Dawn of American Child Nurture* (1970), *American Families: A Documentary History*, edited with Donald M. Scott (1982), *Prefaces to Liberty* (1983), and *Despotism and Democracy: The Great Modern Contest* (2002).

Wishy has taught at Columbia University, where he was a member of the Society of Scholars, and the University of California at Berkeley. He also taught at North Carolina State University from 1973 to 1991.

Since retiring in 1991, he has published three books, including his most recent, *War, the American Way,* in 2009. He is currently working on two books, a conservative history of America and one entitled, *It's Democracy, Stupid.*

Wishy now lives in San Francisco. He is divorced and has two children and four grandchildren.[52]

HARVEY JOHNSON

Harvey Wilson Johnson was born September 26, 1926, in Raleigh, North Carolina. His parents were the late Charles E. Johnson and Nancy White Johnson. His father was one of the founding members of the Sandwich Club.

Harvey was the fourth of four sons: Charles E. Johnson, Jr. (deceased), Richard M. Johnson (deceased), and Bradford W. Johnson.

Harvey is married to the former Katharine Shannon (Trina) Blake.

---

[52] Biographical sketch provided by Bernard Wishy.

They have three daughters: Trina Blanton, Anna Smith, and Jane Brady. Harvey and Trina also have six grandchildren.

He was a graduate of Cathedral High School in Raleigh. He attended the University of North Carolina at Chapel Hill and graduated in 1950. There he was a member of Chi Psi fraternity.

Harvey volunteered for the U.S. Navy in 1944 and served until the end of World War II.

Mr. Johnson was president of Hamlet Ice Company, co-owner of the Charles E. Johnson and Sons Insurance Agency, and later a senior executive of Moore and Johnson Insurance Agency.

He was a member of the Agents Advisory Council, the Fireman's Fund Insurance Company (based in California and subsidiary of the German firm Allianz SE) and the Unigard Insurance Company (based in Washington State and affiliated with QBE of Australia). He is past president of the Independent Insurance Agents of Raleigh, The United Way of Wake County, The Raleigh Little Theater, The Carolina Country Club, The Sphinx Club, and The Terpsichorean Club of Raleigh.

He is a former member of the Jaycees and the West Raleigh Rotary Club. He served on the board of directors of the Chamber of Commerce, the Raleigh YMCA and the Milburnie Fishing Club. He has been active in various fund-raising campaigns including the United Fund, Meredith College, St. Mary's Junior College, the YMCA, and the Salvation Army.

Harvey now resides at The Cypress of Raleigh, a retirement community, at 8821 Cypress Lakes Drive.[53]

HENRY ROYSTER

Henry Page Royster attended the Hill School and entered Princeton University, where he was a member of the freshman and varsity wrestling teams. He was a member of Triangle Club and Tiger Inn. After graduation in 1931 Hank entered the medical school of the University of Pennsylvania. In 1933 he received the MD degree.

In 1938 he married the former Ethel Fisher, with whom he had two children, Louisa Jane and Jonathan Page.

Henry joined the Army Medical Corps in 1942 and was assigned to the 20th General Hospital in Burma as a plastic surgeon. There he earned a Bronze Star and two battle stars. He was discharged as a major.

---

[53] Biographical sketch supplied by Harvey Johnson.

During his 30-year career as a dedicated teacher and plastic surgeon, he wrote a number of research papers. Under his supervision, repair of cleft palates was provided to numerous indigent patients.

A fitting comment made by a friend and colleague summed up Dr. Royster's character: "Uncle Henry was my mentor for many years, and a person whom I have adopted as a role model in surgery. To be accorded the comment that 'he is like Henry Royster' is the highest accolade and compliment that anyone can receive."

In 1975 he retired from the University of Pennsylvania as professor of surgery, emeritus. He came to Raleigh, where he joined the Carolina Country Club and was a frequent golfer.

Henry Royster died June 13, 1999.[54]

REAR ADMIRAL ALEX M. PATTERSON

Alex McLeod Patterson, 91, of 1604 Glen Eden Dr., died in October 1996. He was born on December 13, 1904, in Raeford, North Carolina, son of Martin A. and Martha Jane Monroe Patterson. After attending high school there, he had a year at Davidson College, Davidson, North Carolina, before his appointment to the U.S. Naval Academy, Annapolis, Maryland, in July 1923. As a Midshipman he was a member of the Glee Club and Choir, and played Class soccer. Graduated and commissioned Ensign on June 2, 1927, he subsequently attained the rank of Captain on April 21, 1949, having served in that rank (temporary) from December 1945 until January 1948. He was transferred to the Retired List on July 1, 1958, and advanced to Rear Admiral on the basis of combat citations.

After graduation from the Naval Academy, he remained there until August 1927, for preliminary flight instruction, and was then assigned to the battleship *Pennsylvania*, in which he served as a junior officer for two years. In July 1929 he was transferred to the *USS Oklahoma*, another battleship, and in May 1931 was detached to the *USS Wasmuth*. He continued sea duty in that destroyer until May 1934, when he was ordered to the Postgraduate School, Annapolis, Maryland, completing the course in Applied Communications in May 1936.

He had a month's instruction at the Submarine Base, New London,

---

[54] Adapted from obituary, "Memorials," *Princeton Alumni Weekly,* November 17, 1999.

Connecticut, and in June 1936 joined the *USS Wright*, seaplane tender, to serve until October of the next year. He then reported to the *USS Colorado*, and remained aboard that battleship until June 1940. Prior to and following entry of the U.S. into World War II, he was on duty in the Office of the Chief of Naval Operations, Navy Department, Washington, D.C. and in March 1943 was ordered to duty in connection with fitting out the *USS Oakland*. When that light cruiser was placed in commission, he went aboard as Damage Control Officer and the First Lieutenant, and continued duty in that capacity and as Executive Officer throughout the remaining period of war.

He was awarded the Bronze Star Medal with Combat "V," for "heroic achievement as Damage Control Officer and later as Executive Officer of the *USS Oakland*, during operations against enemy Japanese forces in the Pacific War Area from November 15, 1943, to August 4, 1945...." The citation states further, "Demonstrating sound judgment and foresight, [he] aided in maintaining his ship in a state of combat readiness at all times. As executive officer, he continued to render valuable service in carrying out his important duties as evidenced by the excellent performance of men and material during actual engagements with the enemy...."

In June 1954, he reported as Assistant Chief of Staff for Communications, Joint Staff, Commander in Chief, Carribbean. Two years later he became Professor of naval Science, NROTC Unit, at the University of North Carolina at Chapel Hill, and served there until he retired on July 1, 1958.

In addition to the Bronze Star Medal with Combat "V," Rear Admiral Patterson has the American Defense Service Medal, Fleet Clasp; the American Campaign Medal; the Asiatic-Pacific Campaign Medal with one silver and four bronze stars (nine engagement); the World War II Victory Medal; the National Defense Service Medal; and the Philippine Liberation Ribbon with two bronze stars.

After retirement, Admiral Patterson was on the staff of the N.C. State Department of Archives and History. He set up a program of preservation of county and other local records which were microfilmed for security and research purposes and properly stored. In 1969, he was made a fellow in the Society of American Archivists. Pat also wrote some books on his family's history. He is the author of *The Claro McBryde*, a history of his first wife's family, *The Monroes of the Upper Cape Fear Valley*, a history of his mother's family, and *The Highland Scots, Pattersons of North Carolina and Related Families*.

Survivors of Alex McLeod Patterson included his wife, Bethea Willis Wells Patterson; daughter, Peggy Sabiston and son, Michael Sabiston; son, Alex McLeod Patterson and wife Sybil; granddaughter,

Mary Christie Dees and husband Will Dees and their children, Alexander and Lauren; grandson, Alec and wife Melinda Patterson and their child, Kelsey; stepson, James MacSherry Wells, Jr., and wife, Sharon and their daughter, Catherine, and son, James MacSherry Wells, III; stepdaughter, Matilda Wells Andrews and her husband Jackson Andrews and their two sons, Jackson and MacLeod; stepdaughter, Patricia Wells Coley and her daughter, Leigh and sons, David and Willis.[55]

DR. ARTHUR C. MENIUS, JR.

Dr. Arthur Clayton "Buck" Menius, Jr., 80, died Sunday, October 13, 1996 at Rex Hospital in Raleigh, N.C.

Dr. Menius was born in Salisbury, N.C., on April 30, 1916. He was inspired to study science by a trip to the Engineers' Fair in 1933. He graduated from Catawba College in 1937 and received the Ph.D. in Physics from UNC-Chapel Hill in 1942, doing his research in relativity under John Wheeler. He taught for several years at Clemson University. He came to N.C. State University (then N.C. State College) in 1949 and served as head of the Physics Department from 1956 to 1960. He was one of the team that designed and built the first university nuclear reactor. He served the space program at Huntsville, AL, as a consultant on ballistic missiles.

He was an advocate of nuclear power and helped initiate the academic field of nuclear engineering.

Dr. Menius was named the first Dean of the School of Physical and Mathematical Sciences in 1960. That unit of the university included physics, chemistry, mathematics, statistics, and marine, earth, and atmospheric sciences. He retired in 1981 after serving as Dean for 20 years.

Dr. Menius proved instrumental in the development of the Research Triangle Park and strongly supported the formation of the Research Triangle Institute as a nonprofit organization.

Dr. Menius was a member and deacon of White Memorial Presbyterian Church in Raleigh and belonged to the Carolina Country Club, the Sphinx Club, the Washington (N.C.) Yacht and Country Club, the Esso Regional Discussion Group and the Sandwich Club. He was also a well-known furniture maker, creating authentic antique style pieces for

---

[55] Adapted from obituary, *News and Observer*, Raleigh, North Carolina, October 24, 1996, Sandwich Club files.

his home and for sale. After his retirement, he served as consultant and quality supervisor for a line of reproductions of Tryon Palace Furniture.

He was survived by his wife of 50 years, Lucille Varner Menius, formerly of Chapel Hill; a son, Arthur C. Menius III and daughter-in-law, Becky R. Johnson of Pittsboro; a twin sister, Maude Edna Hilley of Old Lyme, Ct.; and another sister, Tootie Witmer of Tallahassee, Fla.

A memorial service was held on Wednesday, October 16, 1996, at White Memorial Presbyterian Church in Raleigh.

In honor of Dr. Menius and his distinguished service to the College and to N.C. State University, the College of Physical and Mathematical Sciences established the Arthur C. Menius, Jr., Undergraduate Scholarship Endowment.[56]

GEORGE S. SPEIDEL, JR.

George S. Speidel, Jr., Brigadier General, U.S. Army Retired, 86, of 1528 Carr St., died in March 1994. He was born in Pennsylvania in 1907, the son of George S. Speidel and Caroline Blessing Speidel. He graduated in 1931 from the U.S. Military Academy at West Point, N.Y. After graduation he married Tommie Rinehart who died February 24, 1994. They had been together for 62 years. Surviving were two sons, George S. Speidel III of Cincinnati, Ohio, Lt. Col., Retired, Richard R. Speidel of Panama; five grandchildren (one girl who graduated from West Point in 1985); and two great-grandchildren.

Prior to WWII he attended military schools and spent 3 years in Hawaii and four years as an instructor at West Point. He spent WWII in the European Theater and finished as General Patton's G-4 of third Army. He subsequently held many assignments including Bikini, Commandant of the Artillery School at Ft. Sill, Oklahoma, and the Pentagon. He commanded the 40th Division Artillery until he retired from military service in 1961. He obtained a masters degree from Duke University in 1962 and taught mathematics at North Carolina State University for 17 years. During his civilian life he was very active in local organizations including the Retired Officers Association, The North Carolina State University Faculty Club and the N.C. Museum of Art. He was a member of Christ Episcopal Church of Raleigh.[57]

---

[56] Adapted from obituary, *News and Observer*, Raleigh, North Carolina, October 15, 1996, Sandwich Club files.

[57] Adapted from obituary, *News and Observer*, Raleigh, North Carolina, March

KERN HOLOMAN

William Kern Holoman was born in Richmond, Virginia, August 10, 1920. He moved to Raleigh, N.C., as a child and was educated in the Raleigh public schools.

He graduated from UNC-Chapel Hill, June 1942, with a B.A. in English Literature. While a student at UNC, he was elected to Phi Beta Kappa.

Holoman was drafted into the Army in July 1942. He received special training at Rutgers University in French Language and area. After receiving direct commission as 2nd Lieutenant in France in April 1945, he served as Military Government Officer in Germany 1945-1947.

He entered the North Carolina National Guard in 1947 and held numerous staff and command positions for next 30 years. He retired in October 1978 as Brigadier General, Deputy Adjutant General of North Carolina. Decorations and Service Medals include the Legion of Merit.

Holoman's entire business life (1947-1980) was spent as part owner-operator of Boylan-Pearce Department Store in Cameron Village, Raleigh. Numerous managerial positions included Vice-President and Secretary. He was elected "Merchant of the Year" in 1972. In 1980 he sold his business to Rotary District Governor Earl Barnes.

He served numerous civic and service offices and activities in Raleigh. He was also a church officer and Sunday school teacher.

Holoman has been retired since 1980 and his principal interests are travel and reading.

He joined Rotary in October 1968 and his father, father-in-law and older brother were all Rotarians. He held numerous offices and committee chairmanships in West Raleigh Rotary, including serving as President from 1976-77 and District Rotary Foundation Chairman from 1978-82.

In 1982, Holoman led the Rotary District 771 Group Study Exchange Team to India-Nepal-Bangladesh. Kern is very proud of the fact that of the five young non-Rotarians whom he escorted on that trip, four have since become Rotarians.

In 1943, he married the former Katherine Highsmith (deceased 1997). He has four grown sons, three daughters-in-law, nine grandchildren and four great-grandchildren.[58]

24, 1994. Courtesy of the Elizabeth Reid Murray Collection, Olivia Raney Local History Library, Raleigh, North Carolina.

[58] Biographical sketch supplied by Kern Holoman.

GEORGE E. LONDON

George E. London of 2000 Banbury Road died in March 1993.

A Pittsboro native, Mr. London earned a degree in history from the University of North Carolina at Chapel Hill in 1933. He took a job with Carolina Power & Light Co. after graduation, then served four years in the Navy during World War II.

After the war he returned to Raleigh, founded a fuel oil business and started a far-reaching involvement in civic and Episcopal Church organizations.

Mr. London was recognized by the N.C. Literary and Historical Association as the 1991 recipient of its Christopher Crittenden Memorial Award. He served as president of the Carolina Charter Corporation, a not-for-profit organization that has sponsored and financed research in England.

To date, more than 60,000 documents pertaining to colonial North Carolina have been recovered, copied and published in eight volumes called "Colonial Records of North Carolina."

Mr. London served as the president of numerous business and civic groups including the Raleigh Chamber of Commerce, the Raleigh Tourist and Convention Association, the Wake Oil Dealers Association, Raleigh Little Theatre, the N.C. State Art Society and the Raleigh Kiwanis Club. He was named Kiwanian of the Year by the Raleigh Kiwanis Club in 1981 for his long record of local service and community involvement.

He was married to the former Frances Pendleton of Elizabeth City.[59]

GARRETT BRIGGS

I am a Texan, born and raised in Dallas and educated through the Masters Degree in Geology at Southern Methodist University. I received the PhD at the University of Wisconsin and then returned to the South to be an oil field geologist for the California Company (CALCO), based in New Orleans. I subsequently joined the Geology Faculty at Tulane

---

[59] Adapted from obituary, *News and Observer*, Raleigh, North Carolina, March 31, 1993. Courtesy of the Elizabeth Reid Murray Collection, Olivia Raney Local History Library, Raleigh, North Carolina.

University. It was during these first two positions that I became engrossed in costal sedimentary processes such as those occurring on modern deltas and barrier islands along the gulf coast of Louisiana. This is in marked contrast to my doctoral dissertation which focused on ancient abyssal-depth sediments exposed in the Ouachita Mountains of southeastern Oklahoma.

Then it was off to Knoxville, Tennessee, for thirteen years, first as a professor, then Department Head of Geological Sciences and finally as Associate Dean for Research and Resources Development. At the same time my research turned to the application of the knowledge I had accrued about modern deltas and barrier islands to ancient equivalents exposed in the Allegheny Mountains of East Tennessee.

In 1981, I moved to Raleigh to become the Dean of Physical and Mathematical Sciences at NC State. I succeeded Buck Menius, the founding dean of the College and a member of the Sandwich Club. In 1988, and until 1998, I was the President of Peace College, a Presbyterian-related women's college founded in 1857. My principal contribution to the College was to make it a four-year baccalaureate institution. Soon after going to Peace College, someone at N.C. State asked about my whereabouts and was told that I was at Peace to which the enquirer responded, "I didn't even know he was ill."

During my professional career I was, and continue to be, active on civic, church and educational boards which include being President of the Rotary Club of Raleigh, Chairman of the Salvation Army Advisory Board, and Trustee at Shaw University. I served on the vestries of four Episcopal churches, five times as Senior Warden. I am also an Elder of First Presbyterian Church of Raleigh. Before I got so tied up in administration, I authored a number of journal articles and a couple books the most important of which was a book I organized and edited entitled *Carboniferous of the Southeastern United States* published by the Geological Society of America. It was my privilege to be a member of the Sandwich Club and to be a member and past president of the Watauga Club.

Now in retirement and living in the mountains of North Carolina, I am President of the Ashe County Frescoes Foundation (to protect and preserve the frescoes painted in two antique churches here by the world-renowned artist, Benjamin Long). Most important to me, however, is that I can now pursue a life-long desire to be an artist and to paint pictures of the beauty that abounds here.

No bio can be complete without acknowledging my greatest joys:

my wife, Sue, our four children and nine grandchildren.[60]

THOMAS HARTWELL CAMPBELL

Thomas Hartwell Campbell was born on July 27, 1945, in Greenville, North Carolina, into a family of teachers and preachers. His great-grandfather, James Archibald Campbell, founded what is now Campbell University in Buies Creek, N.C. When Tom was three his father left the ministry to go into broadcasting, later founding and leading WNCT-TV, Eastern Carolina's first television station.

Around the age of 13 Tom would go into his room, shut the door and practice introducing his records as if he was a disc jockey. By 16 he obtained his First Class Radio Telephone license and worked part time at a radio station through high school and college. His father didn't like him playing rock and roll music on the radio, suggesting he use a different on-air name. A salesmen at the station suggested he call himself "Tom Terrific," after the cartoon character on the Captain Kangaroo TV show. It stuck.

In 1965, while still a college student, Tom married Elizabeth (Lib) Stroud from Ayden. Declining college grades and a call for help from his father, who then owned WGTM Radio in Wilson, led Tom to drop out of school and join the family radio business. Over the next 24 years he performed every function in a radio station including ownership, but Tom loved writing and voicing daily radio editorials for more than 20 years.

Tom owned and operated radio stations in Wilson, Elizabeth City, Durham, Williamston and Jacksonville at various times. Having sold all his interests in broadcasting he served three years as Executive Director of the North Carolina Public Television Foundation, helping to raise almost five million dollars for new production equipment at our state's public TV network. In 1992, State Treasurer Harlan Boyles asked Tom to become Assistant State Treasurer, providing Tom with an unparalleled education into the inner workings of high-level state government.

In 1996, Tom purchased WRAZ-TV in the Raleigh-Durham TV market. Tom created the TV talk show, NC SPIN, in 1998, producing and moderating a new show each week for more than 12 years that holds the record as the second-longest talk show in North Carolina history. In addition to NC SPIN he writes a weekly column on public policy issues printed by various newspapers across the state.

---

[60] Biographical sketch supplied by Garrett Briggs.

With his son-in-law, Wayne Rivers, Tom co-founded The Family Business Institute, a consulting business to assist closely held corporations. The two co-authored the book, *You Don't Have to Die to Win - Success and Succession for Family Businesses*. In 2003, Tom expanded his company, starting The Efird Bible Study Series, featuring the biblical teachings of Dr. Mickey Efird. These video-based studies are now being used by more than 1800 churches in the United States.

Active in civic affairs, Tom served as president of the North Carolina Association of Broadcasters; president of the Downtown Raleigh Rotary Club, the oldest civic club in North Carolina; and chair of the Wake County Salvation Army Advisory Board. He was awarded the William Booth Award for his service. Tom has also served on the A. J. Fletcher Foundation and the Triangle Chapter of the Juvenile Diabetes Research Foundation boards. He has taught an adult Sunday School class for more than 25 years and served in various capacities in his church.

Tom and his Methodist pastor wife Lib have a grown daughter and son and four wonderful grandchildren. The two serve as leaders of the week-long North Carolina Academy for Spiritual Formation each year as well as a yearly weekend spiritual retreat.[61]

ARTHUR B. MOSS

Arthur Broadus Moss, 76, died Wednesday, November 18, 1988. A memorial service held at Christ Episcopal Church included members of the N.C. Symphony honoring Dr. Moss with a musical tribute.

Dr. Moss held a Doctorate in Business Administration from Harvard University after completion of MBA from Columbia University and an AB in English from the University of North Carolina. His academic positions included professorships at the Darden School of Business Administration, University of Virginia; the Institute pour l'Etude des Methodes de Direction de l'Enterprise, Lausanne, Switzerland; The Amos Tuck School of Business Administration, Dartmouth College; the Institute of Management, Northwestern University; the College of Business Administration, UNC-Charlotte; and Albert G. Myers Professor (emeritus) of Textile Economics and Management, North Carolina State University. Dr. Moss served as a Founding Member of the Board of Advisors of the Graduate School, North Carolina State University.

Dr. Moss's government posts included service as Deputy Assistant

---

[61] Biographical sketch supplied by Thomas Campbell.

Postmaster General, Bureau of Personnel, followed by the position of Director, Manpower Planning and Development during Postal Reorganization (1969-1976). From 1976 to 1978 he served as Director, Office of Management and Finance, Commodity Futures Trading Commission with responsibility for coordination with the Office of Management and Budget and Congressional oversight committees.

In the private sector, Dr. Moss served as consultant to companies that included Swissair, Southern Pacific, Fieldcrest Mills, Hilton Hotels, Western Electric and Union Camp. Publications by Dr. Moss included *Hospital Policy Decisions: Process and Action* (GP Putnam's Sons, 1966) and contributions to management texts and case studies.

Dr. Moss was a member of the Academy of Management, the Strategic Planning Society and the Triangle International Trade Association. His civic involvement included service as Trustee and Secretary of the North Carolina Symphony Foundation; Member, Citizens Advisory Board, Duke University Comprehensive Care Center; Board Member, Hospice of Wake County; President, Triangle Branch, The English Speaking Union; Fellow, N.C. Museum of Art and as an ardent supporter of the cultural arts in the Triangle area. He was a member of Christ Episcopal Church, the Carolina Country Club, the Sphinx Club, the Sandwich Club and the James B. Duke Circle of the Founder's Society.

Born January 13, 1922, in Americus, Georgia, Dr. Moss was survived by two sons from his marriage to Margaret Parker, who died in 1985: Samuel Parker Moss and his wife, Isabelle, of Atlanta, GA and Edwin Alexander Moss and his wife, Marnie, of Los Angeles, CA. Dr. Moss was married to Frances Campbell Reeves of Raleigh in 1987. He was also survived by three brothers, Paul Grady Moss of Atlanta and his wife, Inez, Wade Lansing Moss of Montgomery, Alabama, and his wife, Mildred, and Frederick Watson Moss and his wife, Mary, of Atlanta, GA; five grandchildren; and four step-grandchildren.[62]

JOHN LEWIS, JR.

John Baker Lewis, Jr., was born in Farmville, Pitt County, N.C., on 21 Sept 1936 to John B. and Mary Anderson (Lamar) Lewis. He graduated from Farmville High School in 1954 where he played football and trumpet in the band.

---

[62] Adapted from obituary, *News and Observer*, Raleigh, North Carolina, November 20, 1988, Sandwich Club files.

He received an AB degree in European History from the University of North Carolina in 1958 and an LLB from its law school in 1961.

He served in the United States Navy from 1961 to 1966 on active duty in Japan, in *USS Coral Sea* (CV 43) in the Western Pacific and Viet Nam. He remained in the reserves and retired in 1990 as a Captain.

Lewis married Kay Ellen Isley on February 25, 1967. They have two sons, Benjamin May Lewis and John Thomas Carlysle Lewis both of whom are happily married. His sons have given him two grandchildren each, Margaret May and Maryanna Ellen and Kelan Carlysle and Riley Jane, respectively.

He practiced law from 1966 to 1982 in the firms of Lewis and Rouse and Lewis, Lewis and Lewis in Farmville. Jack served as Town Attorney for Farmville, Fountain and Hookerton. He was appointed a Special Judge of Superior Court by Gov. James B. Hunt, Jr., in 1982 and reappointed by Gov. James G. Martin. He was elected Judge of the Court of Appeals in 1988 and served until 31 Dec 2000.

He has been a public member of the North Carolina Medical Board since 2007. He was chairman of the N.C. Judicial Standards Commission, vice-president of the N.C. Bar Association, the Third District Bar, and was president of the Pitt County Bar in 1971. In addition, he was a member of the Pitt County Historical Society, chairman of the N.C. Property Tax Commission, former member of the N.C. Review of Administrative Rules Commission, a member of the Board of Directors of the N.C. Arts Council, and president and charter member of the Farmville Child Development Commission. He was chosen Man of the Year for Farmville in 1979. Lewis is also a member of Christ Church Episcopal, Raleigh.[63]

A. G. BULLARD, JR.

Amos Gentry Bullard, Jr., was born May 31, 1934, in Person County, the son of A. G. Bullard, Sr. and wife Elizabeth. His father was a prominent educator. A. G. received three degrees from North Carolina State University: B.S. (1956), M.S. (1958), and Ph.D. (1967). The latter two were in Nuclear Engineering.

He received a commission as officer in the U.S. Army and was assigned to the White Sands Missile range in New Mexico. There he

---

[63] Biographical sketch supplied by John B. Lewis, Jr.

conducted studies of nuclear radiation effects. Then he was employed by the U.S. Atomic Energy Commission as a reactor engineer.

On completion of his doctorate he became a professor of Nuclear Engineering at Virginia Polytechnic Institute. His work there included reactor operations and nuclear fuel as well as teaching, research, and consulting.

In 1972 he joined Carolina Power and Light Co. as Manager of Technical and Research Services. Later he was Manager of Research, with responsibility for in-house research and coordination with various agencies. He retired from CP&L in 1993 with 21 years of service.

Dr. Bullard was a member of several committees of the Electric Power Research Institute (EPRI), and a member of many other professional committees.

He is married to Lois Blanchard with whom he has two children, Steven and Elizabeth.[64]

DR. J. ALLEN NORRIS, JR.

Dr. J. Allen Norris of Raleigh, died Tuesday, June 15, 2004, in Sampson County, North Carolina.

He was born in Raleigh, N.C., on January 27, 1937, to J. Allen Norris and Mary Johnson Norris. Dr. Norris graduated from Needham Broughton High School in 1955. He received his BA, MAT, and EdD from Duke University. Prior to receiving the doctorate, Allen Norris taught in the Greensboro public schools for two years. Later he was an instructor in the Department of Education at Duke University. He then accepted a position with Rollins College, Winter Park, FL, where he directed the MAT program and was Provost. In 1976, Dr. Norris became the 22nd president of Louisburg College where he had tenure of 17 years.

Dr. Norris was treasurer/business manager of the North Carolina Conference of the United Methodist Church from 1992 until his retirement in 2002. After retirement, Allen enjoyed teaching Sunday school and Disciple Bible Study and singing in the choir. He served in several capacities at Edenton Street UMC, including Chair of the Administrative Board and the Committee on Staff-Parish Relations. He was active in various capacities of the North Carolina Conference of the UMC. He was a delegate to General Conference and Jurisdictional Conference five times. He also enjoyed spending time and gardening at the family farm, in

---

[64] Drafted from resume provided by A. G. Bullard, Jr., Sandwich Club files.

Clear Run, N.C.

Dr. Norris was preceded in death by his parents and sister, Ann Norris Broughton.

He was survived by his wife of 45 years, Elizabeth "Beth" McLamb Norris and their two children, Betsy Smith and husband, Mike, of Bladenboro and Bill Norris and wife, Anne, of Clinton. He was also survived by five grandchildren, two nieces, and three nephews.[65]

TENNEY DEANE

Tenney Ingalls Deane, Jr., was born in Clearwater, Florida, August 30, 1937. His father was a Presbyterian minister. Tenney graduated from Davidson College in 1959 with a B.A. in Economics. One of his classmates was future governor James Holshouser.

He had a six-month active military duty in 1960 serving with the U.S. Army Security Agency. From 1961 to 1973 he was an account executive with Corporate Insurers Service in Charlotte. In 1968 he served as volunteer "advance man" for Richard Nixon in his unsuccessful bid for president. In 1972 Tenney became deputy campaign manager for Jim Holshouser and when Holshouser was sworn in as governor in 1973, he appointed Tenney to the post of Secretary of Commerce. A short time later he accepted the appointment as chairman of the North Carolina Utilities Commission, where he served until October 1977.

Over the years he was associated with various businesses, some related to natural gas. In April 1988, Deane was appointed chairman of the North Carolina Low-Level Radioactive Waste Management Authority, and later was executive director, until 1990.

Tenney and his first wife Marcella had two children, Tenney III and William; with his second wife Marsha he had two additional children, Henry and Lydia.

He has been a member of many civic organizations, including Rotary Club, Habitat for Humanity, and Raleigh Executives Club.[66]

---

[65] Adapted from obituary, *News and Observer*, Raleigh, North Carolina, June 17, 2004. Courtesy of the Elizabeth Reid Murray Collection, Olivia Raney Local History Library, Raleigh, North Carolina.

[66] Adapted from *News and Observer*, Raleigh, North Carolina, September 2, 1973, November 14, 1973, and November 10, 1976, Courtesy of North Carolina Collection, University of North Carolina, Chapel Hill, North Carolina; also Tenney Ingalls Deane, Jr., resume, 19 August 1993, Sandwich Club files.

BEN PARK

Benjamin Franklin Park was born in 1920, the son of publisher John Alsey Park and Lily Pair Park. His father purchased the *Raleigh Times* in 1911. At age 8, Ben sold newspapers on Saturdays. He attended Myrtle Underwood Elementary School and Raleigh High School (now Needham Broughton). He studied at the University of North Carolina at Chapel Hill, where he played football.

In 1941, his senior year at UNC, he switched from a business curriculum to one in journalism. He was married to Charlotte Eva Miller while in college. They were married for 66 years. They had three sons—Ben F. Park, Jr., Fred Miller Park, and John Alsey Park II.

He joined the Marines in 1942. He had active duty during World War II, with his last assignment in Okinawa. After leaving the service he began work at the newspaper, starting as a reporter, being made city editor, and eventually becoming managing editor. Ben was nominated for a Pulitzer Prize for exposing graft in the city's government. His two older brothers, Albert and John, Jr., also worked on the newspaper.

In 1955, when the *Raleigh Times* was purchased by the *News & Observer*, Park was invited to join the public relations firm of Hill and Knowlton. He stayed with that company for five years. He then formed the Ben F. Park Agency, consulting with clients in the private and public sectors in a one-man public relations company that grew to serve many large regional associations. He helped launch the local chapter of the Public Relations Society of America.

Upon retirement, Ben became the executive vice president of the N.C. Forestry Association. That organization in 1985 sponsored a comprehensive document "Pathways for Forestry in North Carolina." Ben Park was a contributor in planning meetings.

Mr. Park was a member of Christ Episcopal Church, serving on its vestry for many years. He was a member of several clubs, including the Raleigh Ad Club, the Rotary Club, the Sphinx Club, the Terpsichorean Club, the Carrousel Club and the Nine O'Clock Cotillion at the Carolina Country Club.

Throughout his life he was athletic, first in football and Boy Scouts, and later in boating, woodsmanship, and golf. He died on June 19, 2007, at the age of 86.[67]

---

[67] Adapted from obituary, Benjamin Franklin Park, Bryan-Lee Funeral Home,

FRED DeJARNETTE

Fred Roark DeJarnette was born October 21, 1933, in Rustburg, Virginia, which is close to Lynchburg, VA. His father and mother were Daniel Thomas DeJarnette and Inez Virginia Roark, both deceased. He has one brother, William Thomas DeJarnette, who is only 16 months older than him and now lives in Satellite Beach, FL.

His father was an automobile mechanic in Rustburg, but when Fred was the age of two his family moved to Republican Grove, VA, where both parents were from originally. There his parents operated a service station and garage and it was very close to where grandparents lived on farms. After Fred attended the first grade there, his parents moved to Ocean View, VA, in 1942 to work in defense organizations. It was there that his brother and Fred got introduced to model airplanes, general aviation and U.S. Navy airplanes, and it started a passion for flight at all levels.

In order to be closer to his mother's work at the Naval Ammunition Depot in Portsmouth, VA, the family moved there in 1944. DeJarnette attended grammar and high schools there, graduating from Cradock High School in 1952 and also marrying his high school sweetheart, Nadene Dearmon. After high school, he entered Georgia Tech's School of Aeronautical Engineering on the Co-Operative Education program. His co-op job was working at the Norfolk Naval Shipyard in Portsmouth, VA, so he could live at home during his work quarters. During this time Nadene and he had two daughters, Denise and Lisa. Denise Miller is a graduate of Meredith College, has two children, Lara and Ryan Beckwith, and now lives in Wilmington, N.C. Dr. Lisa DeJarnette is a graduate of UNC-CH and is now an M.D. at Wake Med in Raleigh.

After receiving a BS degree in Aeronautical Engineering from Georgia Tech in 1957, DeJarnette continued on to an MS in Aeronautical Engineering there in 1958. He moved the family to Long Beach, CA, to work as an aerodynamics engineer with the Douglas Aircraft Company. He went through the Army ROTC program at Georgia Tech and was called to active duty in 1959 as a 2nd Lt at the Aberdeen Proving Grounds, MD, where he worked with civilians on defense rockets and missiles. After his Army tour he returned to Douglas Aircraft in Long Beach, CA,

www.bryan-leefuneralhome.com, accessed 28 September 2010.

transferred to the Missiles Division in Santa Monica, CA, and then accepted an opportunity to transfer to the Charlotte, N.C., division of Douglas Aircraft Company to work on Army rockets. While there he became acquainted with Dr. Robert Truitt, who was then Head of Aerospace Engineering at Virginia Tech, and also Dr. H A. Hassan, who was a professor in the same department. He soon developed a passion to return to graduate studies for a PhD degree, so in 1961 he entered Virginia Tech as both a graduate student and a half-time assistant professor in the Aerospace Engineering Department with Dr. Hassan as his advisor.

Within a year after arriving at Virginia Tech, Dr. Truitt left to become the Head of the Mechanical Engineering Department at N.C. State College and shortly afterwards Dr. Hassan left to join Dr. Truitt's Department. Together they developed an Aerospace Engineering program and changed the name of the department to Mechanical and Aerospace Engineering and N.C. State College later became N.C. State University. DeJarnette completed his course work at VA Tech in 1963 and then went to NASA Langley Research Center to perform his PhD dissertation while a member of the Mathematical Physics Branch under the leadership of Dr. Leonard Roberts. DeJarnette completed his PhD degree in 1965 and accepted the position of Associate Professor in Aerospace Engineering at Virginia Tech. While there he continued research with NASA Langley and served as acting Head of Aerospace Engineering from 1967 to 1969. During this time he participated in a NATO 8-week summer research program in Calgary, Canada (1968) and the NASA/ASEE summer faculty program at NASA Ames Research Center (1969).

In 1970 DeJarnette accepted an offer to join the Mechanical and Aerospace Engineering Department at N.C. State University where he is currently a full Professor. He teaches and performs research in aerodynamics with the NASA Langley Research Center. From 1987 to 1992 he served as the Director of the NASA Center of Excellence in Hypersonic Aerodynamics at N.C. State University. From 1989 to 1994 he served as the Director of the NASA Mars Mission Research Center at N.C. State University. He served as Head of the Mechanical and Aerospace Engineering Department from 1994-1999. He currently serves as Campus Director of N.C. Space Grant Consortium and Liaison Professor for the National Institute of Aerospace (NIA) in Hampton, VA. DeJarnette's awards include the following: R. J. Reynolds Award for Excellence in Teaching, Research & Extension (1988-1993); O. Max Gardner Award (1990); Graduate Alumni Distinguished Professor, NCSU (1990-1992); American Institute of Aeronautics and Astronautics (AIAA) Thermophysics Award (1995); Fellow in AIAA (1996); Fellow in NIA

(2004); and Alexander Quarles Holladay Medal for Excellence at NCSU (2005).[68]

JOHN C. MARTIN

Chief Judge John C. Martin was born in Durham, North Carolina, on November 9, 1943. He received his B.A. and J.D. degrees from Wake Forest University, and has completed the General Jurisdiction Program at the National Judicial College in Reno, Nevada, and the Justice Executives Program at the University of North Carolina at Chapel Hill. Following his legal education, Judge Martin served as an officer in the United States Army from 1967 through 1969, and was in the private practice of law in Durham for thirteen years, where he served on the Durham City Council, chairing the City's Public Works Committee. Judge Martin was Resident Superior Court Judge for the Fourteenth Judicial District (Durham County) for more than seven years before his election to the North Carolina Court of Appeals. He has served on the Court of Appeals for more than twenty-one years, including more than seven years as Chief Judge. He is admitted to practice in all State and Federal courts in North Carolina, the United States Court of Appeals for the Fourth Circuit, and the United States Supreme Court.

In addition, Judge Martin has served as Chairman of the North Carolina Judicial Standards Commission since 2001. In that capacity, he drafted legislation to reorganize and expand the Commission and implement improved procedures for investigating and processing complaints of judicial misconduct. The legislation was enacted by the General Assembly in 2006 and became effective January 1, 2007. He is a member of the Chief Justice's Commission on Professionalism and its Executive Committee, and is a member of the North Carolina Judicial Council.

Judge Martin has been active in the field of judicial education in North Carolina, having participated in the development of the concept of establishing a statewide judicial college to provide training and continuing professional education to court officials and employees at all levels of the North Carolina court system. Judge Martin then served, by appointment of the Chief Justice, as a member of the North Carolina Judicial Education Study Committee, which planned and implemented the establishment of the North Carolina Judicial College as a part of the School of Government at the University of North Carolina at Chapel Hill. He serves as a member

---

[68] Biographical sketch supplied by Fred DeJarnette.

of the Judicial College Advisory Committee, and participates in providing training for attorneys, trial judges, and appellate judges in the fields of judicial ethics and professionalism.

Judge Martin is a member of the Wake County Bar Association (vice-president, 1997-1998; chairman, Administration of Justice Study Committee, 1992; Endowment Committee, 2004-present) and the American Bar Association (Appellate Judges Conference, Judicial Division Ethics and Professionalism Committee). He is a member of the Council of Chief Judges of State Courts of Appeal and has served on its Education, Finance and Executive Committees. Judge Martin has been a member of the Wake Forest University School of Law Board of Visitors since 1987, and has served two terms as a member of the Wake Forest University Alumni Council, as well as a member of the Parents Advisory Councils of Wake Forest University, Appalachian State University, and Chatham Hall School.

Judge Martin is married to the former Margaret Rand of Durham and has three children, two step-children and four grandchildren.[69]

PARKER CHESSON

J. Parker Chesson, Jr., was born August 19, 1941, in Hertford, North Carolina. He received his B.S. degree magna cum laude in biology from East Carolina University in 1963, and also an M.A. in Education and Biology in 1964. He earned the Ph.D. from North Carolina State University in 1974, majoring in Education and Zoology.

At the College of the Albemarle in Elizabeth City he proceeded from Assistant Professor of Biology in 1964 to Chairman of the Department of Mathematics and Physical Sciences, to President of the College, a post he held from 1975 to 1992.

Parker served the N.C. Department of Community Colleges for four years, finally joining the Employment Security Commission in 1996.

He has been involved in many North Carolina public service organizations. To name a few: the Coastal Resources Commission, the Marine Sciences Council, and the Association of Community College Presidents.

Dr. Chesson received several honors including the Governor's Award for Distinguished and Meritorious Service in 1984, and the Distinguished Alumnus Award from the Department of Education and Psychology of North Carolina State University in 1995.

---

[69] Biographical sketch supplied by John C. Martin.

Parker is married to the former Wynda Chappell of Belvedire, N.C. They have two daughters—Daphne Lynn and Melanie Anne.[70]

THOMAS McGUIRE

Thomas H. McGuire was born in 1948. He received a B.A. degree in Music from Emory University in 1969, where he was elected to Phi Beta Kappa. In 1975 he obtained the Ph.D. in Musicology from UNC-Chapel Hill and an M.B.A. from there in 1978. His first position for two years was with Continental Oil in Houston. He then became Executive Director of the Arkansas Symphony Orchestra.

In 1982 Tom became the first Executive Director of the North Carolina Symphony Orchestra. After six years, he took the executive director position with the A. J. Fletcher Foundation, involving The Fletcher School of Performing Arts and the National Opera Company. He remained there for fifteen years

McGuire was the recipient of the City of Raleigh's 2003 Medal of Arts Award.

Since 2003 Dr. McGuire has been associated with the philanthropic advisory group Armstrong McGuire, which advises on the management of non-profit charitable organizations, including information on fund-raising.

Tom has been on and continues to serve on many charitable boards and committees. Tom has served as chair of Leadership Triangle, treasurer of the Greater Raleigh Convention and Visitors Bureau, secretary of The Stewards Fund, and member of the advisory board of the Lucy Daniels Foundation. He is past president of Hilltop Home, a residential care facility for handicapped children, and has served on the boards of Ravenscroft School, Saint Mary's School, the John Rex Endowment, the N.C. Center for International Understanding and the Rex Healthcare Foundation. He has served as leader on several visits to foreign countries in behalf of the Center for International Understanding. Included were Russia, France, and Spain.

Tom is married to the former Barbara Hunter. They have a daughter, Martha.[71]

---

[70] Adapted from resume provided by J. Parker Chesson, Jr., Sandwich Club files.

[71] Adapted in part from Armstrong McGuire Philanthropic Advistory Group website http://www.amapag.com/v.php?pg=28, accessed 5 June 2010, and a resume provided by Tom McGuire, Sandwich Club files.

JAMES STEWART

James E. (Jim) Stewart was born in High Point, North Carolina, grew up in Davie and Forsyth Counties, and graduated from Clemmons High School. He married his high school sweetheart, Norma Jones, and has two sons and two daughters plus twelve grandchildren. Jim enjoys sports and most outdoor activities (gardening, landscaping, hiking – taking his grandchildren tent camping in the N.C. mountains every July), reading, writing, history, and antiques.

Jim served in the U.S. Army; basic training at Ft. Jackson, SC; parachute training at Ft. Benning, Ga.; and 77th Special Forces (Green Beret) at Ft. Bragg, N.C. He obtained the rank of Sergeant First Class during his Service.

After discharge from Service, Jim studied civil engineering at N.C. State College while married and raising two boys. While at N.C. State, Jim worked many part time jobs, including N.C. State's Security department and two years with U.S. Geological Survey. Upon graduation in May 1961, he worked at the State Highway Commission and N.C. Office of Water Resources (now DENR). He began consulting engineering with Moore - Gardner and Associates, Asheboro, NC.

Jim later moved to Jacksonville, N.C., and went into business with Land Surveyor L.T. Mercer, eventually owning the company. James E. Stewart and Associates provided Consulting Engineering, Land Surveying, Land Planning for local, state and federal governments, public utilities, private corporations and the construction industry.

He has held elected and appointed offices in Jacksonville and Onslow County. He is a dedicated Christian and church member, having served in many positions including Chairman of Administrative Board, Board of Trustees, and Sunday School teacher.

Jim has been active in Engineering and Surveying societies, serving as President of Consulting Engineering Council of N.C. and President of the Central Chapter of Professional Engineers of N.C. He is a Life member of PENC, NSPE, ASCE, AWWA, and the N.C. Society of Surveyors; a long time member of N.C. Society of Engineers; and has served on the Surveying Advisory Committee of Coastal Carolina Community College.

He served N.C. State on the Alumni Board, Engineering Foundation Board, the Engineering Advisory Council, NCSU Athletic Council and the N.C. Forestry Foundation Board.

Jim is a 45 year member of Rotary International with 37 years perfect attendance and has served most club and district committees. He has served as Jacksonville Club President and District 773 (southeastern N.C.) Governor. He has attended many District Conferences, four International Conventions, and seven Zone Institutes. He and Norma are Paul Harris Fellows, and he is a Rotary Foundation Benefactor.

Jim is also a dedicated member of the Sandwich Club.[72]

DR. JAMES C. McNUTT

Dr. James C. McNutt is currently the President and CEO of the National Museum of Wildlife Art in Jackson Hole, Wyoming. He is a museum professional with experience in university, state, and nonprofit governance and over twenty years experience producing major exhibitions of over $1 million, festival events, and funding campaigns. He works closely with clients to identify high-quality programming, secure sponsorships, and reach out to community audiences. He brings in-depth knowledge of planning, fundraising, budgeting, technology integration, and facility development, to the creative tasks at the heart of museums and arts organizations.

Most recently Dr. McNutt led the development of the nation's newest united arts fund in San Antonio. He helped community leaders raise operating funds, recruit the board, hire an executive director, and organize the inaugural fundraising and community awareness campaign. In 2004 he completed an operations report for the Admiral Nimitz Foundation (Texas) that helped win $9 million worth of bond financing to expand the National Museum of the Pacific War.

Dr. McNutt was President and Executive Director of the Witte Museum in San Antonio from 1999-2004. His leadership led the Witte Museum to create a Water Resource Center, merge with a neighboring museum, and save a much-loved circus collection for San Antonio. He led fundraising of $1.2 million for a national exhibit that gave the museum its first climate-controlled gallery, completing a $600,000 renovation in less than eight weeks. During his tenure the amount of annual fundraising doubled and memberships increased by 33%.

Prior to moving to San Antonio, he was Director of the North Carolina Museum of History in Raleigh. Successes there included one of the earliest Internet distance learning programs in the country for

---

[72] Biographical sketch supplied by James Stewart.

museums. He implemented a team approach to exhibit development that resulted in the award-winning *Health and Healing Experiences in North Carolina*, a \$1 million project. Previously he was Director of Research and Collections at the University of Texas Institute of Texan Cultures where he led research teams covering diverse disciplines, exhibition and program development, and a variety of publications, including books, newsletters, audiovisuals.

Dr. McNutt completed a three-year term on the Board of Directors of the American Association of Museums in 2006 and frequently speaks to professional, business, and civic groups throughout the country. He received a Bachelor of Arts degree at Harvard with honors in English before achieving a Master's in English and a Ph.D. in American Civilization at the University of Texas at Austin.

Dr. McNutt's professional and client work includes: Alamance Co. Historical Museum, Bexar County Arts and Cultural Fund, La Grange Redevelopment Foundation, National Museum of the Pacific War, National Museum of Wildlife Art, North Carolina Museum of History, University of Texas Institute of Texan Cultures, Warsaw Veterans Celebration Foundation, Winston-Salem Public Library, and the Witte Museum.[73]

ROBERT A. BARNHARDT

A native of West Pittston, PA., Dr. Robert A. Barnhardt had a long and successful career in higher education associated with the textile industry, including a close relationship with industry as well.

He earned a B.S. degree in Textile Engineering from the Philadelphia College of Textiles and Science (now Philadelphia University), an M.S. from the Institute of Textile Technology, and a Masters of Education and a Doctorate in Higher Education Administration from the University of Virginia.

Barnhardt's work experience includes Chairman of the Department of Textiles at PCT&S, and a 22-year association with the Institute of Textile Technology serving as Dean, Executive Vice President and Chief Operating Officer, and President. Over a period of 20 years at North Carolina State University, he served as Dean of the College of

---

[73] Drafted from Arts Consulting Group, "James C. McNutt, Ph.D., Senior Advisor," http://artsconsulting.com/june28/pdf_bios/bio_mcnutt.pdf, accessed 4 February 2011.

Textiles, Interim Vice Chancellor for Academic Affairs and Provost for 6 months (2003) and Interim Chancellor for 6 months (2004). During these years, he gave over 125 invited lectures in the U.S., Europe, and the Far East. However, his greatest enjoyment was teaching at both the undergraduate and graduate levels for 46 consecutive years.

He was active in many professional associations including the establishment of the National Textile Research Center where he served as the first Chair of the Operating Committee, the Accreditation Committee of the Textile Institute of the United Kingdom where he served as its initial Chairman, the National Council for Textile Education where he served as President, and was one of two invited U.S. members of the GEDRT (Groupe Europeen d'exchange d'experiences sur la Direction de la Recherche Textile). He was also a Board member of the Foundation of the Curry School of Education at the University of Virginia as well as an officer of the Alumni Association of North Carolina State University.

Throughout his career Barnhardt was active in many industry associations including the American Textile Manufacturers Institute (ATMI), the North Carolina Textile Manufacturer's Association (NCTMA), the Southern Textile Association, AMTEX, and Harriet and Henderson Yarns.

His contributions to education and the industry have been recognized with honorary membership in the National Golden Key Honor Society and Phi Kappa Phi Scholastic Honor Society. He is a Fellow of the Textile Institute (United Kingdom) and was awarded the Institute Medal. He has been recognized by the Young Menswear Association with its AMY award for Industry Leadership and Achievement. In 2008 he was awarded the Watauga Medal by North Carolina State University.

At the local level, Barnhardt has been active in Rotary International, serving as President of the Rotary Club of West Raleigh and in various church activities including singing in the choir.

He always looked forward to and enjoyed the friendships of Sandwich Club Members as well as their stimulating papers.[74]

RAY LONG

William Ray Long was born April 7, 1934, in Hartsville, S.C. He graduated from University of North Carolina at Chapel Hill in 1953 and received a law degree from UNC in 1959. There he was a member of the

---

[74] Biographical sketch supplied by Bob Barnhardt.

Tau Kappa Epsilon fraternity. On graduation he began work with Branch Banking and Trust in the trust department.

Branch Banking and Trust (also known as BB&T), is one of North Carolina's oldest banks and a leading originator of residential mortgages in the Southeast. In addition to deposit accounts and loans, the company offers insurance, mutual funds, discount brokerage, wealth management, and financial planning services. Business services include leasing, factoring, and investment banking.

Ray married Mary Caroline Lewis June 17, 1967. They have three children: Anna Caroline, Holley Whitehurst and William Ray Long, Jr.

Ray rose to become the Chief Trust Officer for BB&T which position he retained until his retirement in 1998.

A committed Episcopalian, he served until December 2001 as Treasurer of the Diocese of North Carolina. He is an active Rotarian.[75]

THOMAS HARRELSON

Thomas Joseph Harrelson was born February 1, 1941, in Brunswick County. His father was a grocer and farmer. "Tommy" received an undergraduate degree from University of North Carolina in Chapel Hill and a Masters degree in business administration from the Wharton School of the University of Pennsylvania.

After working for the Caltex Oil Company for two years in New York and Switzerland, Harrelson returned to Southport as a partner in his father's business. He was involved with the community of Southport.

In 1970 he ran for the House of Representatives for Brunswick and Columbus Counties, and served two terms. In 1987 he was appointed Deputy Secretary of Transportation by Governor James Martin. In 1989 he became DOT Secretary, holding that post until 1993. During that period he oversaw the start of a major road-building program.

Since then he has been a governmental affairs consultant, serving as lobbyist for various business and governmental interests in the North Carolina General Assembly and local governments. Also, he has worked as consultant for the U.S. Navy and for the engineering firm Earth Tech.

Thomas is married to Julie Ann Harrelson and they have two daughters and two grandchildren. Julie Ann is retired from CP&L.

Harrelson has been very active in civic affairs. He recently served as chairman of the Triangle Transit Authority Board of Trustees, spent

---

[75] Adapted from biographical information on Ray Long, Sandwich Club files.

time on the Triangle World Affairs Council Board, and was chairman of the ITRE Council. He was a member of the Raleigh Rotary Club and the Southport St. Philips Episcopal Church.

In 2009 Tommy and Julie Ann moved from Raleigh to Southport, where he established a group like the Raleigh Sandwich Club.[76]

HENDRIK STRUIK

Hendrik (Henk) Struik was born June 21, 1940, in Schalkhaar, The Netherlands. He is the only Sandwich Club member born in another country. He was number 8 of 10 children.

Henk received the B.A. (equivalent) in International Business at Nijenrode, The Netherlands in 1963. He then obtained a B.A. in Economics at the University of Michigan in 1964 and an M.B.A. in 1965 at Michigan.

He was married to Edith Louise Foley on June 6, 1964, in Ann Arbor, Michigan. They have two married sons—one in Chicago and one in Carlsbad, CA—and a married daughter in Raleigh. They have seven grandchildren.

From 1966 to 1994 Henk worked for Eli Lilly & Company, most recently in the International Division. His last position was Director of Operations for Middle East, Near East, Africa & Mediterranean Basin, based in Geneva, Switzerland.

Henk has a number of outside interests, as follows: Edenton Street United Methodist Church—various leadership positions; Rotary International—member of West Raleigh Rotary; MentorLink International (Board)—ministry to pastors in the developing world; and Neighbor-to-Neighbor (Board)—mentor to students from inner city projects.[77]

BILL JENKINS

My full name is James William Jenkins, Jr., but my nickname is Bill (Billy to my childhood friends and fishing buddies). My Dad's name was Jim and my son's name is James so I got stuck being called by my middle name. I was born in Roanoke Rapids on May 15, 1956, where the

---

[76] Adapted from biographical information on Thomas Harrelson, Sandwich Club files.

[77] Adapted from biographical information supplied by Henk Struik.

only thing I can remember is going to see the trains as they came roaring through town.

My family moved to Morven, then to Southern Pines and finally to Raleigh when I was ten years old. We were following my Dad's career as he moved up the public school ladder, first as a teacher, then principal, then superintendent and finally, Director of Early Childhood Education in the big City of Raleigh.

I attended school in Raleigh, graduating from Sanderson High School in 1974. Somehow, I got accepted to NCSU and studied Landscape Design and got my degree in 1980. I became registered as a Landscape Architect in 1989 and then decided that I also needed my Professional Engineering license, so with a combination of additional education and self-study, passed the PE exam and was registered as PE in 1997.

I have two children, James and Hannah. I finally found true love later in life and married Pam on Valentine's Day 2004. Together, we blended a new family with step-kids, Leah and Charlie. James has graduated from college and is struggling to make a living as a musician, while the other three kids are still in college.

I work for a consulting engineering firm where I manage our North Carolina operations, focusing on transportation and heavy civil engineering works. Our company does a lot of highway and bridge design work for Departments of Transportation throughout the southeast.

I was a member of the Sandwich Club for about two years, but had to give it up due to travel considerations associated with my job. I thoroughly enjoyed my association with the Sandwich Club and sincerely miss the friendship and camaraderie of the group.

My current interests include rehabbing our 20 year old home, fishing (especially salt water fishing), traveling, and boating.[78]

DONALD R. WEISENBORN

I was born in Los Angeles, California, on May 25, 1944. I am married to the former Joyce Ann (Joanne) Padgett of Hendersonville, N.C., and we have one daughter, Kimberly, who lives in Raleigh with her husband Dr. William F. Durland, Jr., and our three grandchildren, Will, Zoe and Elizabeth.

I have more than 35 years of technical management, consulting and planning experience primarily in the electric utility industry. I am

---

[78] Biographical sketch supplied by Bill Jenkins.

experienced in transmission, generation, and system planning; transmission engineering and construction; system operations; transmission maintenance; and asset management. I retired from Progress Energy in February 2002 after 29 years, and since that time I have been an independent contractor/managing associate with ScottMadden, Inc. While employed by Progress Energy / Carolina Power & Light Co., I held several technical management positions, including Manager of Transmission Engineering and Construction, Energy Control Center Manager, and System Planning Manager. I have been a member of and held positions within numerous electric utility organizations including the Electric Power Research Institute (EPRI), the Institute of Electrical and Electronic Engineers (IEEE), the Southeastern Electric Reliability Council (SERC), and the Edison Electric Institute (EEI). I am a Registered Professional Engineer in North Carolina (#007757). As a Managing Associate with ScottMadden, I advise national and international clients on process development/improvement, strategic/business planning, organizational design, engineering audit, and asset management matters.

I hold a BS in Electrical Engineering from Old Dominion University, Norfolk, Virginia (1972); and a Masters in Management from Duke University's Fuqua School of Business, Durham, North Carolina (1976).

Community service interests include volunteer and financial support for: Habitat for Humanity, Meals on Wheels, Food Bank of N.C., Wake County Schools, Loaves and Fishes, Stop Hunger Now, and Wake Tech. I am long standing member and Past President of the Rotary Club of West Raleigh.[79]

PERRY L. GRADY

Dr. Perry L. Grady was born on September 10, 1940, in Duplin County, North Carolina. He received his B.S. and M.S. degrees in Electrical Engineering, as well as the Ph.D. in Fiber and Polymer Science, from North Carolina State University. He is a member of Sigma Xi, Phi Kappa Phi, Eta Kappa Nu and Phi Lambda Upsilon honor societies.

Dr. Grady is emeritus Associate Dean of the College of Textiles and Professor of Textile Engineering, Chemistry and Science at North Carolina State University. He is currently the Director of Business Development at the American Association of Textile Chemists and

---

[79] Biographical sketch supplied by Donald Weisenborn.

Colorists in Research Triangle Park, North Carolina. He has taught courses and conducted extensive research in textiles in the areas of materials, fiber production and properties, instrument and control system design and development, computer applications, energy utilization and conservation, electrotechnology applications, ballistic protection and garment and textile care. He is a registered professional engineer with over eighty publications to his credit. Dr. Grady has worked extensively with industry as a consultant and through numerous industry-partnership programs at NCSU. He is co-editor of the books *Microprocessors and Minicomputers in the Textile Industry* and *Automation in the Textile Industry: From Fibers to Apparel.*

Dr. Grady is a member of the Fiber Society, The American Association of Textile Chemists and Colorists, APICS – The Educational Society for Resource Management, The Institute for Electrical and Electronic Engineers, The Textile Institute, and ISA – The Instrumentation, Systems and Automation Society. He is a fellow of ISA and has served as Director of the Textile Industry Division and in numerous other local, regional and national officer positions. He has served as Chairman of the Board of ISA Services, Inc. (a for-profit subsidiary of ISA), a member of the Executive Board and as Vice President for the Publications Department of ISA. He served as President of ISA from 1999 to 2000 and as a member of the Executive Committee and the Executive Board from 1998 to 2001. He continues to serve as chair and member of several ISA committees. He is a member of the Board of Directors of the North Carolina Agribusiness Council. He has also served on the Board of Directors of the Triangle Universities Computation Center, as founding Director of the EPRI Textile Office, and as a founding Co-Director of the Industrial Electrotechnology Laboratory. He is an Honorary Board member of the Hohenstein Institute in Germany. He served as a member of the Governing Council of the Fiber Society from 2002 to 2004. Dr. Grady was coordinator for the design, construction and occupation of the new College of Textiles twenty-three million dollar complex that was completed in 1991. He has visited more than 150 academic, industrial, and government facilities in the U.S., Canada, Europe, Asia, and South America. He has participated in developing national and international standards with ATMI, ANSI, and ISO. He has served as chair of the ISO/TC72/SC7 subcommittee on "Data Interfaces for Monitoring and Control of Textile Machinery." He is a member of AATCC committees RA 43 on Drycleaning and RA 105 on Supercritical Fluids. He has served as a member and chair of program, department, college and university committees.

Dr. Grady has received the Outstanding Extension Award at North Carolina State University, the Fiber Society Distinguished Achievement Award, the ISA Textile Industry Division Achievement Award, and the North Carolina State University College of Textiles Cates-Rutherford Lecturer and Distinguished Alumnus in Fiber and Polymer Science Award.

Perry Grady married Patricia Whitman on June 17, 1962. They have two girls, Patricia Lynn who married Thomas Clark Moore and Julie Anne who married Brian James Mock. They have five grandchildren ages 1-15.[80]

ZANE FINKELSTEIN

Colonel Zane Finkelstein is a soldier retired. He was born in Knoxville, Tennessee, in 1929. His education included Castle Heights Military Academy, Lebanon, TN, and high school in Rochester, NY. Finkelstein earned his JD from the University of Tennessee in 1952.

Zane married Rosemary Morgan in 1953.

After being drafted (1954) and commissioned in the Judge Advocate Generals Corps, U.S. Army, Colonel Finkelstein served as trial council, defense council, claims officer, legal assistance officer and Soviet liaison officer in Berlin, Germany; Military Trial Judge in the 82nd Airborne Div.; Assistant Professor of Law at West Point; Chief, Status of Forces Agreement negotiator and CIA investigator in the Republic of China; Chief, Tort Branch, the Judge Advocate General's Office, the Pentagon; Staff Judge Advocate, Cavalry Division, Vietnam; Chief of Criminal Law instruction, the Judge Advocate General's School and adjunct at the University of Virginia Law School.

Col. Finkelstein attended the U.S. Army War College. After a term as Judge, U.S. Army Court of Criminal Appeals, he became the Legal Advisor and Legislative Assistant to the Chairman of the Joint Chiefs of Staff.

Following his assignment to the Chairman JCS office, he was Theater Judge Advocate in the Republic of Korea. Then he taught at the Army War College and as an adjunct at Dickinson School of Law, Penn State and Temple Universities.

Upon retirement and for 10 years, Col. Finkelstein became first International Counsel and then General Counsel and advisor of the president BMY Division, Harsco Corporation. He culminated his

---

[80] Biographical sketch supplied by Perry Grady.

professional life as Vice President and General Counsel, JA and Associates, a consulting firm doing business in China and Korea.

Zane Finkelstein and his wife Rosemary have two sons. One son has a PhD in optics, living in Tucson, Arizona, where he helps maintains an empty nest for his son working in Madison, Wisconsin, and his daughter, a freshman at Davidson. The other son is a JD practicing law in Raleigh where he is rearing his daughters, ages 10 and 7.

Colonel Finkelstein has been decorated several times for merit by the United States, the Republic of China, and the Republic of Korea. He was once decorated for valor. He has been a Boy Scout Commissioner, chair of the Carlisle Area Religious Counsel, a vestry member, a leader in St. John's Outreach Commission and an active member in Rotary, the VFW, Military Officers of America, Association of the United States Army and the American Legion. He served on the board of several non-profit corporations, including the Army War College foundation where he Served as Editor-in-Chief of the AWC Press and is a member of the Bar of the United States Supreme Court, the Tennessee Supreme Court, the U.S. Court of Military Appeals, the Federal Claims Court and several circuits.[81]

---

[81] Biographical sketch supplied by Zane Finkelstein.

Index

Page numbers in boldface type indicate images.

E

Jack Ellis 6, 24, 37-38

F

Fadum, Ralph 10, 25, 57-59
Finkelstein, Zane 26, 113-114

G

Gatton, Harry **22**, 25, 70-71
Geoghegan, George 12, 16, 25, 55-56
Gill, Edwin 11-12, 19, 21, **22**, 24, 35, 53-55, 78
Grady, Perry 26, 111-113

H

Hamilton, Alfred 7, 9, 21, **22**, 25, 63
Harrelson, Thomas 4-5, **23**, 26, 108-109
Hickman, Addison 10, 24, 53
Hicks, V. M. 9, 24, 35-36
Holoman, Kern **23**, 26, 89
Hunter, John **22**, 25, 76-77

I

J

Jenkins, Bill 26, 109-110
Johnson, Charles E. 5, 16, 24, 29, 30, 62, 83-84
  History of the Sandwich Club 6-13
Johnson, Harvey 25, 30, 83-84
Johnson, Ted 6, 16, 24, 41-42
Jones, H. G. **22**, **23**, 25, 27, 75-76
  Comments 21

K

L

M

N

O

P

Q

R

S

T

U

V

W

X

Y

Z